# UNWANTED
# SPY

# UNWANTED
# SPY

## The Persecution
## of an American
## Whistleblower

## JEFFREY STERLING

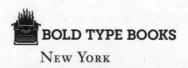
BOLD TYPE BOOKS
NEW YORK

Bold Type Books
116 East 16th Street, 8th Floor New York, NY 10003
www.boldtypebooks.org
@BoldTypeBooks

Printed in the United States of America
First Edition: October 2019

Published by Bold Type Books, an imprint of Perseus Books, LLC, a subsidiary of Hachette Book Group, Inc. Bold Type Books is a co-publishing venture of the Type Media Center and Perseus Books.

The Hachette Speakers Bureau provides a wide range of authors for speaking events. To find out more, go to www.hachettespeakersbureau.com or call (866) 376-6591.

The publisher is not responsible for websites (or their content) that are not owned by the publisher.

Print book interior design by Linda Mark.

Library of Congress Control Number: 2019938818
ISBNs: 978-1-56858-557-4 (hardcover), 978-1-56858-558-1 (e-book)

LSC-C

10 9 8 7 6 5 4 3 2 1

*To the love of my life, Holly.*
*You have given more meaning to this journey*
*than I ever hoped to discover.*

Who am I?
I am the ghetto child,
I am the dark baby,
I am you
And the blond tomorrow
And yet
I am my one sole self,
America seeking the stars.

**from Langston Hughes, "America"**

# Contents

# A Note About Names

THIS IS A TRUE STORY, BASED MAINLY ON MY OBSERVATIONS and recollections, supplemented in a few places by information drawn from public sources. The people who appear in these pages are a mixture of public figures (such as journalist James Risen and CIA director George Tenet) and many private individuals. In most cases, the specific identities of the private individuals are not important for you to understand the themes and meaning of my story. Therefore, I've chosen to refer to them by pseudonyms, as indicated by the use of quotation marks around their names when they are first mentioned (as with my childhood friend "Arnold," for example). In some cases, I have omitted or changed places and names after the CIA's Publication Review Process. In other cases, I have chosen to leave their redactions blacked out.

# Prologue
## Waiting for the Verdict

WHERE AM I? HOW DID I GET HERE? THOSE ARE THE KINDS of thoughts you have when your ultimate nightmare comes true.

It was January 26, 2015, my second long day of waiting in a small, windowless, soundless conference room just outside courtroom number five on the fourth floor of the federal courthouse in Alexandria, Virginia. Over the past two weeks, I had been on trial, accused of violating the century-old Espionage Act.

As an undercover officer for the Central Intelligence Agency, I'd been involved in Operation Merlin, a covert scheme to derail the Iranian effort to build a nuclear bomb by providing their scientists with fake, flawed blueprints for warheads, channeled through a Russian scientist. Operation Merlin had ultimately backfired when the Iranian experts detected the fraud, as revealed in the book *State of War* by reporter James Risen.

Agency leaders were furious—not at themselves, for launching a risky and ill-conceived scheme, but at the author who'd dared to expose their incompetence. In their eagerness to punish someone for their embarrassment, they looked around for a scapegoat. They found me. A compliant US attorney dutifully filed an indictment charging me with "Unlawful Retention and Unauthorized Disclosure of National Defense Information, Mail Fraud, Unauthorized Conveyance of Government Property, and Obstruction of Justice"—nine criminal charges in all, based on the claim that I'd supposedly leaked classified information about Operation Merlin to James Risen.

The truth is that I did not leak any classified information related to CIA operations to James Risen, or to anyone else. But I am a whistleblower. I'd blown the whistle by suing the CIA for discriminating against me when I was an employee there. I'd also attempted to blow the whistle about the dangers of Operation Merlin—not by leaking, but by submitting my warnings to staff members of the Senate Intelligence Committee.

Sadly, those warnings were ignored. I'd been forced to accept some disheartening truths: that neither blatant discrimination nor a dangerous operation related to weapons of mass destruction were matters of real concern to the powers that be at the Agency or among the members of Congress charged with oversight of intelligence matters.

Even before the trial had begun, I'd known that my prospects weren't good. The world had witnessed the cases of Edward Snowden, Chelsea Manning, John Kiriakou, and a series of other whistleblowers whose prosecution—some said persecution—had been pursued by President Barack Obama with an eagerness that almost suggested a personal vendetta. In the atmosphere created by these cases, the mere accusation of having leaked classified information was enough to automatically condemn someone. In refusing to plead guilty and instead insisting on my right to go to trial, I knew I was facing an uphill battle. But I could not and would not confess to something I did not do.

During the trial, the government did not present a shred of hard evidence to validate the charges against me. Even Judge Leonie Brinkema summarized the case against me as being based on "very powerful circumstantial evidence" rather than on hard proof.

But there was one incriminating fact about which there could be no doubt. The CIA had paraded a whole host of current and former agents in front of the jury, and I didn't look like any of them. I was a black man who'd dared to try to build a career serving my country as an officer of the CIA.

The trial had lasted a week and a half. Now I was enduring the most excruciating part of the whole ordeal: waiting for a verdict.

How the hell did it all come to this?

I'd grown up as a true believer in the American dream. Work hard, do your duty, and stand up for yourself—those were the rules of the game, or so I'd been taught. I knew I'd done nothing wrong, and I knew that fighting against wrongs is what an American hero is supposed to do. That's all I knew how to do. That's why I was now clinging to hope and continuing to fight—unable to comprehend how defending my rights could somehow get me branded a traitor.

Thankfully, I wasn't alone in that waiting room. My wife, Holly, and my attorneys, Ed MacMahon and Barry J. Pollack, were there beside me. But having company isn't very comforting when you have no words to say to one another. Silence can be uncomfortable, and when it's forced it can be absolutely nerve-racking. All of them, especially Holly, had believed in me and fought for me, and I could tell that awaiting the jury's decision was almost as excruciating for them as it was for me.

But for me there was a sharper twist to this agonizing time of uncertainty. More than waiting to learn my fate, I was waiting to learn what my country thought of me.

This was a question I'd wrestled with my entire life. The experience was often stressful, even painful. My entire life had been one of fighting against stereotypes, assumptions, and limitations placed on me because of the color of my skin—something that happened to me repeatedly in both white America and black America. The American dream I believed in and strove for wasn't a white American dream or a black American dream. It was simply *my* American dream. But to many of those around me, it must not have been the right American dream—because I kept getting into trouble, through no intention of my own.

That, in a nutshell, is the story of the events that brought me to this room. My years of struggling to find a place in American society where I could be accepted for who I am. My battle to be recognized as a worthy member of the CIA. My shadowy conflict with people within the Agency who, for some reason, were unwilling to accept me as part of the team. The ways racial prejudice continually blocked my efforts to contribute to a cause in which I deeply believed. And, finally, the strange and unfounded accusations of having betrayed the country that I love.

These memories swirled aimlessly in my head during the long hours of waiting. The room itself was lifeless and almost empty. It was dominated by a table too big for the room, on which lay only a few discarded copies of the *Washington Post* and an abandoned paperback of the novel *Life of Pi*, left behind, I suppose, by some previous defendant in an earlier trial. The book seemed eerily appropriate. I'd enjoyed the movie, which had vividly conveyed the message that sometimes the reality of a situation can be so horrible that having a more hopeful version to hang on to may be necessary to make life more tolerable—"the relativity of truth," as one critic wrote.

Wasn't that my whole story, from the beginning?

As the second day of deliberations dragged on, the silence was broken occasionally by calls into the courtroom to hear about requests from the jury members. Once they wanted clarification about some aspect of the judge's instructions; another time, they asked to review a piece of evidence. Then, most hopefully, the jury informed the judge that they were deadlocked on at least some of the nine charges against me. Judge Brinkema suggested they continue with their deliberations after taking a break for lunch.

Maybe there was a chance that the American system of justice would come through for me at last. But by this time I was numb to everything, unable to get excited one way or the other. The deadlock just meant more waiting.

Holly, Ed, Barry, and I had barely settled back into the lifeless room after a quick lunch when we were told that the jury had reached a decision. My heart sank. I had a queasy feeling that I knew what was coming. We returned to the courtroom.

As the members of the jury filed back in, I noticed they avoided looking in my direction. *It's like a scene from a movie*, I thought. I glanced back at Holly sitting behind me, and I noticed that a couple of marshals had entered the courtroom. I gave Holly the strongest smile I could, and I felt the love she poured out to me in return. When Judge Brinkema asked me to rise, I stood as straight and tall as I could manage, flanked by Ed and Barry.

The clerk began to read aloud the verdicts to the nine charges against me. The first time I heard the word "guilty," something went numb inside me. I know the same word was repeated eight more times, but I didn't hear it. I could only hear Holly crying, her sobbing becoming louder with each sentence from the clerk. At the moment, I felt nothing for myself, but my heart was breaking for her.

I noticed Judge Brinkema motion to "Mr. Hart," the courtroom bailiff. He'd been kind to us in that courthouse every day, and I could see the hesitation in his eyes as he walked over to Holly and asked her to compose herself. At the same time, the marshals moved into position right behind me. *Are they going to take me away from Holly right now?* I wondered. Somehow that was the only thing on my mind.

I remained as composed as possible as Judge Brinkema congratulated the jury on their work and dismissed them. Much to my surprise—and to the surprise of just about everyone else in that courtroom, including the marshals—she did not order me into custody. Instead, with an unaccustomed note of gentleness in her voice, she set a date three months in the future for me to return for sentencing.

For the moment, I was free to go.

As we walked out of the courthouse, I didn't know what to think. I had been found guilty of a crime I didn't commit. The nightmare I had feared and fought against my entire life—being accused and judged merely because of the color of my skin—had come to pass. All I knew was that I had to hold on tight to Holly, who was still sobbing by my side. As we walked down the courthouse steps with the cameras of news reporters and television crews focused tightly on us, I tried to offer her a smile. It wasn't easy. So I squeezed her hand even tighter.

When the two of us settled into the car for the long drive home, the numbness in my brain began to thaw.

I realized that there was something strangely, sickeningly comforting about what had just happened to me. I'd finally gotten an answer to the question I'd been wondering about my whole life: *What does my country really think of me?*

I didn't like the answer. But at least it clarified for me what I had to do now. I thought back to the *Life of Pi* on the table in the waiting room. *Life of Jeffrey*, I thought. My next job was to find some more palatable version of reality to cling to in the face of a devastating and painful truth.

I didn't think it would be hard to do. One way or another, I'd been doing it my entire life.

# PART ONE

# ROOTLESS

# CHAPTER ONE

# Child Without a Village

I AM THE SEVENTH OF SEVEN SONS BORN TO HELEN AND HOW-
ard Sterling—six lived, one son was stillborn. In order, we were Michael, Steven, Robert, Mark, John, and me, Jeffrey. Growing up, I was
proud to be the youngest son of a strong mother. I dreamed we were
like the powerful family of Texas oil tycoons in the TV show *Dallas*.
But my dreams were the closest thing to a real family I ever had. I was
in a large family, but I never felt a part of it.

Unlike my brothers before me, I was born via cesarean section and
in a different hospital—although one would think that by the time I
came along, the way would have been clear enough for me to be born
in the normal fashion. My mother constantly reminded me of the toil
and pain I'd put her through. "They cut me open to get you out," she
would exclaim, displaying the scars she would bear forever. My brothers taunted me with claims that I wasn't a real Sterling—that I'd been
found on the doorstep or dropped off by aliens.

In my heart of hearts, I wished it was true.

Somehow it seemed as if I'd come along too late to be a true member of the family. Around the house, I saw plenty of pictures depicting family gatherings, trips, and celebrations, but nothing like that ever happened during my life. The clan had largely scattered before my arrival. Michael and Steven had already left our home in Missouri for military service, while Robert and Mark were back and forth from their places in California. As for John, he loved torturing me with constant put-downs, teasing, and physical abuse.

When they were around, as much as I wanted to be close to them, I was afraid. These were the only male figures in my life. I wanted so badly to gain their approval, and I was so terrified at the prospect of not being accepted.

From what I could see, or at least what I thought I saw, each of my brothers seemed to be living in ways I couldn't help but admire. Michael was in the navy and traveled around the world; Steven was a tough and dedicated marine; Mark and Robert were hardworking family men; John was a basketball star, seemingly bound for college. I gained a sort of confidence in myself and what my future could turn out to be as I observed them.

There was no father because he'd abandoned our mother when I was five years old. So, for male role models, my brothers were it. And, Michael, the oldest, was the one I especially looked up to. When I was in grade school, I was always giddy with excitement when my mother announced that Michael would be visiting home. I was so proud and envious of him. He was out there seeing and experiencing the world— not only outside of our hometown of Cape Girardeau, Missouri, but outside of the country. Whenever he was in town, I did my best to make sure he picked me up from school. I carried his service pictures with me to school and bragged endlessly that my brother, the one in the navy, was coming to get me. I made sure he arrived just before the school buses departed. I couldn't have had a better audience than school buses brimming with kids who didn't have brothers as worldly as mine. I would have preferred he wore his uniform, but I could never convince him to do that.

It didn't matter where we went or what we did while Michael was in town, I just wanted to be near him, to hear of his travels throughout the world as a man in the navy. Michael was always good for tantalizing yarns about his exploits. He was too late for any action in Vietnam, but he was on a ship that sailed in the region just as the conflict was drawing down, and he sailed to various ports of call in Africa and other exotic locations that I yearned to see. I couldn't help but be mesmerized; he provided me with the perfect window on the world and a fantasy of escape. Michael became the only father figure I would ever have in life. It was not surprising that I was always in tears when it was time for him to leave. As I look back, I have to wonder whether he knew the impact he had on me as a child.

Sadly, in the years to come, the promise in Michael and all of my brothers would turn to personal disappointment as I witnessed each of them struggling through life's difficulties and perils. Michael and Steven never made lasting careers of military service, Mark and Robert never seemed to establish themselves or their families, and John never went to college. The larger-than-life images I saw in my brothers were torn down. I didn't know whether to feel sad or angry at my brothers for their difficulties, for what I couldn't help but consider to be their shortcomings. It may have been unfair of me to place so much reliance on them as role models. But the reality of my situation thrust them onto that pedestal. It was evidently a pedestal they neither understood nor wanted. And when they ultimately became more human than god-like to me, I could no longer view them with the same childish innocence and awe.

Then there was my mother. Everyone in our hometown affectionately knew her as Miss Helen. She was not only the matriarch of the Sterling family, she was also a mother figure for many in Cape. Miss Helen would never turn anyone away who needed assistance, whether in the form of food, money, or a place to stay for a while until they could get on their feet again. She was adept at taking care of older folks whose children had long forgotten them, and she joyfully took personal interest in assisting young single mothers coping with the rigors of parenthood, admonishing them to get off the streets and instructing them on providing a home for a child, especially when the father was of little or no help. Clearly, this was a challenge she knew something about, and everyone looked up to and respected her for her kindness.

Miss Helen worked as a municipal court clerk. Her official duties included preparing the court docket and collecting traffic fines and fees. Her unofficial duties included being an informal advisor for the community. Time after time, individuals facing new court summonses or an arrest warrant would flock to Miss Helen for guidance. Instead of giving legal advice, she gave instruction on what to expect and how to act: "Don't miss your court date. Act like you have some sense and are willing to face up to your responsibility. Stand up straight and look at the judge. Stop saying 'you know' to the judge."

Miss Helen was the only constant in my life, and if I could say I was close to anyone as a child, it would have been her. I wanted for nothing material growing up: I had a roof over my head, clothes on my back, food on the table, and toys for Christmas. I admired the way she provided a household for her sons despite the absence of a deadbeat father. And she did her best to instill in me a sense of pride and self-esteem. She did this in small ways—for example, by constantly reminding me to use proper English and especially to avoid hateful words like "nigger"—and in big ways, by urging me to stand up for myself, even in the face of prejudice and contempt. For all intents and purposes, she was my mother and my father.

However, there were times when my admiration for Miss Helen felt wasted. There were so many occasions where I felt as if I had to compete with everyone else for her motherly affection and attention. It was a sort of estrangement that made no sense to me and always left me with an empty feeling when dealing with her. Strangers treated her as if she was their mother, and, in my heart, I felt she was more of a mother to everyone else. Maybe this can explain why I could never call her "mama" or any other less-formal term than "mother."

Yet I did everything I could to be a son to her. I was the kid who stayed home all the time, never ran the streets, and always earned excellent grades in school. Miss Helen always knew where I was and what I was doing. On the nights she worked late, I would wait up until I knew she was safely home. Seeing some of the angst she experienced with my brothers, I felt I at least owed it to her to not be a burden. One particular episode was dreadful for me as I heard her frantic pleas for one of my brothers, who was acting out publicly, to settle down so as to avoid attracting the attention of the police: "Please, please come inside. They're going to kill you! Please come in the house!" At those moments, I felt helpless for her, but all I could do was be her son.

Miss Helen didn't return my devotion. Despite my best efforts, she seemed to come down hard on me for the slightest transgression. There was the summer evening when, feeling bored, I took a ride on my bike. I liked riding my bike during the humid summer nights. The streets were silent, and the darkness obscured all the dangerous sites that I normally shied away from during the day. It was around 10 p.m., and I was riding aimlessly around and around the neighborhood when I decided to stop where a group of other kids had gathered under a streetlight about three blocks from my house. I recognized them and they me, but none of us really knew a thing about one another. I was just an innocent bystander trying to fit in, laughing at their jokes and being amazed at their stories under that bright light, with bugs flying about and crickets crooning.

Suddenly an old drinking buddy of my mother's approached. "Jeff!" he commanded with a slight slur to his speech. "Your mother said get your ass home."

My streetlight companions burst out laughing, ending any hope I had of being accepted by the group. I turned away and walked my bike home the three blocks with my head down in shame. When I reached the house, Miss Helen was standing on the porch, glaring down at me with a chilling look of disapproval. I passed her without a word and went straight to bed.

Of all the members of my family, my mother is the only one I had any feeling of genuine love for—which made my later disappointment with her even deeper.

As for my father, he was basically a mystery to me. When Miss Helen mentioned him, I would often say, "I don't even know what he looks like."

Her answer was always the same: "You should, 'cause you look just like him."

The similarities evidently didn't stop there. Whenever I became hotheaded, as kids sometimes do, my mother would say, "You're just like your father." I didn't know exactly what she meant about my father's temper until years later, after I'd moved away from Cape. On one of my return visits home, when my mother was holding court with a group of her friends in the living room, someone mentioned how abusive men can be to their wives. Another person chimed in, "But when a man forces his wife to have sex, it ain't rape. That's the law!"

That prompted Miss Helen to get up on her soapbox. "Of course a woman can be raped by her husband," she declared. "It happens all the time. Howard raped me every time he touched me. All of my kids were the product of rape." She said it with a cruel sort of matter-of-factness that tore right into me.

Hearing her, and feeling as though the eyes of everyone were now on me, I could only muster, "Well, that certainly makes me feel good. Thank you."

I think her statement had an especially intense effect on me because I was the youngest child in the family. My parents' relationship must have been near its end when I was conceived, which makes the likelihood that I was the product of one of the worst forms of violence that can be inflicted upon a woman even greater. Something about me and the way I viewed my position in the family changed forever.

Comments by my brothers deepened my feelings of estrangement in regard to my father. Steven, Robert, and Mark all lived with our father in Los Angeles at one time or another following our parents' separation. When they separated, Howard moved to California and Miss Helen stayed in Cape. While she was happy to be free of Howard and his controlling and demeaning ways, she frequently let me know how heartbroken she was when the judge presiding over their divorce gave Steven, Robert, and Mark the choice of whether they wanted to live with Howard in sunny California or remain with Miss Helen in Cape. The promises of the beach and Disneyland were too much for my brothers, and they naturally chose to leave Miss Helen for a less-than-ideal life with Howard. When asked about life with Howard, they would reply, "That nigger is evil, pure evil. Don't let him get his hooks into you. He's a liar, and he will try to take advantage of you."

As for me, I never saw my father, although I occasionally spoke to him on the phone. I didn't believe he could be as bad as my mother and my brothers made him sound. Or maybe I just didn't want to accept the possibility that a man like that could be my father.

>‹‹

PROVIDING THE BACKDROP for this family was my hometown. Cape Girardeau is a hamlet about ninety-nine miles south of St. Louis, nestled along the western banks of the Mississippi. If you've heard of Cape, it's probably because the right-wing radio host Rush Limbaugh was born there, which in its own way tells you a lot about the town.

Cape is the kind of place Mark Twain wrote about, and I doubt it has really changed much since the days of Huck Finn. It is a quiet town, save for the occasional wailing fire truck and the flashing lights of a police car pulling over a speeder. There is no smog, no bright neon lights. There is a band shell in the park for evening concerts in the summer, a perfect setting for taking the family with some lawn chairs, a blanket, and a cooler full of drinks and snacks. On Independence Day and other holidays, there are parades with proud school marching bands, clowns, fire trucks, and Shriners motoring around in brightly colored miniature cars paying homage to fallen veterans. Cape also has the typical county fair with dilapidated rides and prize livestock contests, as well as a sampling of local cuisine interspersed among the usual carnival fare of corn dogs, cotton candy, and funnel cakes. Cape is the type of town that closes down at night. When I was a youth, no one was expected to do anything on Sundays save for going to church. The blue laws made sure that nothing was sold on Sundays except for food.

Not only is religion the spiritual foundation of Cape, it is also an institution of racial division. Blacks go to black churches and whites go to white churches. I can never remember a white face in the churches I attended—although I never had much inclination to attend church beyond the excursions forced upon me by my mother. They thankfully ended around my early teens, when I found watching pro sports a better way to spend a Sunday.

The racial divisions in Cape affected much more than the churches. I lived part of my early childhood in a neighborhood called Marble City Heights, a hilly area in the central part of Cape. Unlike in other neighborhoods, the houses in the Heights were typically wood framed rather than brick. Some of the houses were nice, elegant homes, while others looked like a mishmash of materials found along the side of a highway and nailed together to form a ramshackle structure that would never pass a housing inspection.

One such house was the one next door to mine, where "Miss Emily" lived. It had siding in several mismatched colors, old wooden windows, flaking paint, and an assortment of junk strewn about the yard. Miss Emily was a rotund elderly woman of diminutive stature with pulled-back bluish-gray hair and a dark complexion. She had the typical features of the female elders, with knee-highs, false teeth, and a motherly face weathered and battered through the years. Known as the neighborhood watchdog, Miss Emily spent most of her day sitting on the porch observing all the goings-on in the neighborhood. Her house sat on a bit of an incline, so it seemed as if she and the house were looking down as you passed by. "Hi, Baby, how you doin'? Y'all stop messin' 'round in that street. Don't make me get off this porch!" were the constants bellowed by Miss Emily up on her throne. I was always amazed at the strong voice coming from such a frail-looking elderly woman. If one didn't respond with a "Hi, Miss Emily," or "How you doin', Miss Emily?" her radar seemed to go up and she kept an even keener eye out for any misdeeds you might be up to.

There was always respect for the elders of the neighborhood, which generally meant anyone with gray hair. The elder women were always greeted as "miss" and the men were always addressed as "mister." Last names were rarely used. Not addressing an elder appropriately was almost as blasphemous as cursing in front of one's parent.

Even though the occasional ice cream truck rolled through the streets, most of the neighborhood kids got ice cream from "Mr. Sam." Typical of the male elders, Mr. Sam was a tall, light-skinned man with a plump belly and suspenders to hold his pants up. He had a wood-framed house that, like Miss Emily's, was thrown together from random scraps of material. It was on a hill just above mine and hidden from public view by bushes and overgrowth. Mr. Sam sold ice cream from a big freezer on his enclosed front porch. He also sold an assortment of candy inside a small glass case. I pressed my face against that glass many a day, ogling the goodies inside. Like many of the elders, Mr. Sam knew everyone in the neighborhood. He made a point of knowing exactly what a patron's usual purchase was.

Another area of Cape was Smelterville (usually pronounced something like "Smothahville"), a low-lying area right along the river. Like the Heights, Smelterville was predominantly black. All of the homes in Smelterville were downhill from the main road, where the pavement ended and the streets were gravel. It reminded me of the swamps I had seen on televised nature programs. The people of Smelterville seemed more southern to me than anyone else in Cape. The men I saw there typically wore overalls, while the women would have on flowered dresses and have their hair wrapped up in large handkerchiefs. The children were usually barefoot, and their clothes always seemed soiled. There was always a stray dog or cat wandering through the abandoned cars sitting alongside the houses.

When the city planners built the floodwall to protect the town, they did not extend it as far as Smelterville. As a result, Smelterville was notorious for being periodically decimated by floodwaters. The houses there were all propped up on stilts of some kind, either wood or stone blocks. However, this protection was never enough against the raging Mississippi, so the houses in Smelterville were in even more desperate condition than those in the Heights. Possibly because of the periodic flooding, there was always a particular smell associated with Smelterville—a dank, almost sweet odor that permeated the air and everything in the neighborhood.

The only reason I spent time in Smelterville was because my mother had friends there and liked to go to Porter's, the local bar. I became quite familiar with Porter's, as she usually took me along for social visits and occasional parties. It was a dark sort of place at the bottom of a graveled hill. There was a long vinyl-covered bar banked by swiveled bar stools and neon beer signs that provided just enough light for the tables that were scattered about the room. There was a jukebox, a pinball machine, a couple of small pool tables, and an area big enough to dance. I always liked going to Porter's with my mother because it was the one place I knew that had moon pies. As she socialized, I made my pick of either a chocolate or a banana moon pie. The owner of the bar would occasionally give me a couple of quarters to play the pinball machine. In those days, pinball machines were set up with five balls per game as opposed to three. With my moon pie and pinball games, I would be happily occupied for a good amount of time and of no concern to my mother or any other adult there.

Then there was the last neighborhood I lived in, on South Middle Street. There were paved streets with sidewalks, streetlights, and no wooded areas. There were one or two wood-framed houses, but most of the houses were properly constructed of brick; they had basements and often a second floor. To me, coming from the Heights, these houses seemed like stately manors, and the move felt like going from the country to the city. However, just a couple of blocks over were the same sort of shacks I was used to seeing in the Heights.

To my amazement, most of the inhabitants of South Middle were white. This was the first time I had ever come so close to white folks. They had clearly been in that neighborhood for years, as they were all senior citizens who rarely ventured out of their houses. Apparently, they had missed the last "white flight" train taken by the middle-class refugees who'd abandoned that part of Cape years earlier.

The dark side of the neighborhood was a block away on the cross street, Good Hope. Whenever I heard about people "out on the streets"—including my brothers—I immediately thought of Good Hope. There were a couple of bars and a few scattered businesses, like a barbershop and machine-tool plant. People were always just standing around with forty-ounce beers or liquor bottles wrapped in brown paper bags or dragging on concealed joints. There was usually a craps game happening right out in the open, with the gamblers' yells of confidence alternating with anguished cries of defeat.

One year, my school bus stop was on Good Hope, and while waiting for the bus I would notice the broken bottles and bloodstains adding color to the street. Good Hope was where I saw the drunks and winos. There was a difference between a normal drunk and a wino. A normal drunk typically drank beer or whiskey, got drunk on the weekends, and went home to sleep it off. A wino drank wine of any variety and usually of low quality—brands like Mad Dog 20/20, Night Train, and Boone's Farm, among others. The wino was always drunk and constantly reeked of alcohol. The wino would never make it home. At their drunkest, the winos were staggering down the street aimlessly or passed out in puddles of their own urine.

Good Hope had a loudness I was not used to. Shouting and screaming from brutal fights or arguments was normal. I rarely saw police cars until I lived near Good Hope. In the early years, the police officers were always white, so their very presence on Good Hope was the epitome of white authority and a source of notable tension.

Living near Good Hope gave me a sense of what people meant by the word "ghetto." However, my feeling was I didn't live in the ghetto; I just lived near it. For me as a child, my home, the house on South Middle, was my world. I considered it my sanctuary, a safe haven from a dangerous world I didn't belong to. But, my mother being the type of person she was—renowned for her prowess in the kitchen and the fact that she never turned anyone away—there were constant intruders into that haven. Miss Helen loved to entertain guests with a lively game of poker, a game called "bid-n-whiz" (at least that's the way it sounded), or just sitting around, talking about whatever, over the background music from forty-fives on the record player. The one constant for any visitor was alcohol. Visitors would always bring beer, which my mother enjoyed, or something harder.

Though I detested the constant flow of visitors, I did notice how my mother was at her best with a house full of people. Those were the times she looked happiest. It was not so much from the alcohol, but because she enjoyed having people around.

Since I was always home, I took notice of everyone who came by. I kept my distance from them all, but I also stayed close enough to make observations. I trusted no one and took every opportunity to get back at them for intruding upon my fortress of solitude, especially when it came to the hard drinkers.

One of the visitors who would often come by was "Joe," an old friend of my mother's. As a wino, Joe preferred to drink cheap wine, but my mother wouldn't allow him to bring that into her house. Instead, he would usually bring a bottle of Old Grand-Dad or some other strong drink that I considered little better than paint thinner. Joe always had a suit jacket on, regardless of whether it matched the rest of his ensemble.

Joe was always a source of entertainment for the household. When he was drunk, he would get quite emotional. Whenever the song "Misty Blue" was played on the record player, Joe would burst into tears. His wife had died many years earlier, and I think that song made him think of her and how much he missed her. It was quite a pathetic sight, this slobbering drunken man with tears streaming down his tightly closed eyes, mumbling his love for a long-departed wife over and over again.

One day, when Joe was passed out in a chair in our living room, I saw a great opportunity for mischief. I placed one receiver from my toy walkie-talkie behind a curtain just above Joe's head, and positioned myself with the other receiver in the next room so I could watch him undetected. In the deepest voice I could muster as a ten-year-old, I said, "Joe . . . This is God, Joe."

In his drunken haze, Joe stirred and mumbled, "Yes, Lord, I hear you."

Holding back my laughter, I continued more sternly, "Joe, you have to stop drinking. Joe, you have to stop drinking."

With his eyes closed and clutching his hands, Joe said, "I know Lord, but life is so hard, it's so hard." He began to cry.

"It's okay, Joe, you will be okay. But please stop drinking," I commanded. With his head down and his eyes still clenched shut, Joe raised his hands and said, "I hear you, Lord! I will stop drinking." He then collapsed back into the chair and resumed his slumber.

Given his reaction, I sort of felt bad, but this was a drunk invading my home. Of course, he was back the next week, passed out in the same chair.

I found an escape in television. It showed me that there was a whole different, more pleasing world out there, and I longed for it. I didn't see the television world as fantasy; it was more real and endearing to me than Cape. I spent hour after hour in front of the television not only watching, but also learning. When there were only the three network channels, I sat absorbed in *Hee Haw*, *Barnaby Jones*, *Quincy*, and the ABC movie of the week. *Mutual of Omaha's Wild Kingdom* was my favorite nature show. There was no zoo in Cape, so that show was the closest I could get to seeing animals in the wild. I was fascinated by the different countries and cultures, especially when Jim Fowler ventured through darkest Africa in pursuit of big game.

When cable television arrived, the extra channels expanded my world beyond belief. News programs were my favorite. Walter Cronkite and the *MacNeil/Lehrer NewsHour* became mainstays of my evenings. I still remember watching a special news report about how some man was resigning his job as president. The adults around me saw the news story in racial terms—"See how white folks are!"—but I found it interesting. Later, I took particular interest in the events of the Iran hostage crisis. Every day, I was glued to the set for updates, watching a president's administration being destroyed by events beyond his control in a faraway foreign land.

Television provided the life tutors I lacked in reality. My idea of what it was to be a man came from watching Sidney Poitier movies like *In the Heat of the Night*; *To Sir, with Love*; and *Guess Who's Coming to Dinner*. When I watched Poitier proudly declare, "They call me Mr. Tibbs!" I knew that this was the sort of black man I wanted to be.

Other shows epitomized family life for me. I liked to imagine the members of my own family affectionately saying good night to one another the way each episode of *The Waltons* ended. And I longed for a loving mother and father who bonded with one another using humor like the husband and wife in *The Jeffersons*—so different from the stinging insults and put-downs that passed for humor in my family.

Besides television, my other favorite pastime was going down to the Mississippi River, just a few blocks from the house on South Middle. I loved watching the majestic riverboats slowly making their way through the murky water, as well as the barges carrying mysterious cargo to unknown destinations. I spent hours imagining where the river could take me in the world: down past New Orleans, into the Gulf of Mexico, and from there to the Atlantic Ocean and the world beyond. In between daydreams, I practiced skipping stones. It was quite a personal accomplishment to make a tenner on the choppy Mississippi—though there was no one for me to share the accomplishment with.

Life for me was like being on an unguided tour, seeing a lot of things but with no one to explain them to me. Seemingly of no interest to anyone in my family or my hometown, I merely faded into the background like a nondescript stranger. For all intents and purposes, I was not really there—more like a ghost drifting through life than a flesh-and-blood member of a larger society.

# CHAPTER TWO

# Neither Black nor White

M ISSOURI WAS THE LAST STATE TO OFFICIALLY ABOLISH SLAV-
ery, and a stubborn refusal to abandon the old ways was certainly reflected in the mind-set of Cape Girardeau's inhabitants, white
and black. The Cape I grew up in was starkly divided along racial lines.

When I was growing up, there were few places where blacks and
whites intersected. They made chitchat in the shops sometimes, but I
rarely saw much more than that. Countless folks would visit my mother's house, but only a handful of whites ever crossed her doorstep.
When one did, it usually meant trouble of some kind, often involving
the police.

I don't think I saw more than a handful of white kids until I reached
middle school, which in Cape started in seventh grade. Although all
the grade school kids of the town converged at that point, the middle
school was integrated in appearance only. We arrived and departed on
different buses, the lunchroom tables were strictly divided by color,
and the playground looked like a sort of modern art painting, with
distinct fields of separate colors, never blending.

For me, the one exception to this normal separation was my friend "Arnold." Arnold lived a few blocks from my house on South Middle, and looking back I realize that he must have been what folks thought of as white trash, because he lived suspiciously close to a black neighborhood. We met for the first time at May Greene, one of the principally black primary schools in Cape, and Arnold became my first best friend. We began spending a lot of time together—riding bikes, sharing toys, and doing all the normal things that childhood friends are supposed to do. I never thought of Arnold as "my white friend." The only thing I really noticed was how his house had a different smell than mine. It always reminded me of a *Sanford and Son* episode where Fred Sanford, played by Redd Foxx, commented that "white folks' houses don't have any smell in them!" Despite the lack of flavor in his house, we got along just fine.

One day when I was about eight or nine, it dawned on me that Arnold was really different, at least in the eyes of others. He and I were wrestling in my front yard when a couple of older black guys from a neighborhood even rougher than ours walked past. One of them gazed upon us with a look of pure contempt. "Look at that shit!" he exclaimed, and snorted with disapproval. Somehow I understood what he meant.

I suppose that was the day I started paying attention to the differences between black folks and white folks. I noticed that Arnold's skin was lighter than mine and that he had freckles, something I'd never seen on a black face. His hair was straight and just lay flat on his head, not kinky like mine.

I also began to understand that there were things that black folks did and things that white folks did. I learned that black folks don't eat lasagna or pasta like white folks do; that black folks cook with lard, while white folks cook with vegetable oil; and that black folks eat catfish and fried chicken, while white folks prefer lobster and oysters. White folks like to have surgery and fly in planes, while black folks don't do such foolish things. And only white folks can be racist, not black folks.

The differences went on and on. What was confusing to me was that they were only cosmetic, with no real substance at all. What difference did it make that white folks ate in a different way or listened to different music? Over time, I was to learn that it made all the difference in the world.

My biggest source of information about those differences was what the black folks had to say about white folks when they were hanging out on our porch or on Good Hope in the middle of the day. They'd be drinking as usual, and sooner or later someone would start singing the same old song: "Why try to have something in life when white folks won't let the black man have nothing? White folks is ornery. I ain't working for no white man." It was clear to me that they regarded white people as evil, plain and simple.

A rumor went around for a while that white men were putting a chemical in soft drinks that made black men sterile. I remember asking, "How come this thing affects black folks, but not white folks?"

"Oh, they know how to do it," I was confidently assured. "They *know* how!"

There was also a story about BK sneakers, which were popular with the black kids. Supposedly they had a hidden message imprinted on the sole that only became visible when the sole was worn out: "Thank you for buying our product, *Nigger*!"

It all sounded completely insane to me, but these were the kinds of things I heard about white folks all the time.

I did see an air of superiority in the behavior of whites that seemed to confirm some of what I'd been hearing. It was quite common to hear white folks refer to blacks as "porch monkeys" or "coons." One time, at my first job as a bagger at the local grocery store, a white child no more than ten years old bounded up to me and said, "Hey, boy!" His family, whose groceries I was bagging, looked at me with a sort of pride. I responded by walking away, leaving their remaining groceries for another bagger.

Another time, a white shopkeeper announced that he didn't want any niggers in his convenience store and gave me quite a beating. I had never been called a nigger before, and I was shocked and angry. On my way home, hurt and tearful, I imagined how my brothers were going to teach that man a lesson once they found out he'd put his hands on me. I told my family, but to my surprise, they didn't do anything.

In other cases, the prejudices of white people were expressed more subtly. For example, when I became a teenager, white people could usually be counted on to start a conversation with me by asking, "What sports do you play?" I was a damned good student and would rather have been asked, "What's your favorite subject in school?" But that never happened.

Despite these experiences and the everyday comments by black folks, I just couldn't accept the idea that all white folks were evil. To me, the biggest evil I could associate with Cape's whites was their seemingly oblivious attitude toward inequities in the world, particularly when it came to those experienced by black folks. The whites I encountered firmly believed that there was no such thing as racism, and if blacks were ever treated unfairly, it was their own fault.

I decided it was important for me to think for myself about the issue of race, and to not accept anyone's opinions without examining the evidence for myself. I began trying to follow this path at an early age.

I remember, as a grade school kid, turning to my mother for answers to some of the questions I had about race. "Mother," I asked her, "why are some people prejudiced against others?" I had learned that word "prejudiced" from watching television.

She took a sip of her beer and continued flipping through a magazine without looking up. Finally, she said, "Well, Jeff, some people are like that. They just don't know any better." Her answer was the most evenhanded and color-blind comment I had ever heard. I had to wonder whether she really meant it or was just appeasing a curious kid.

"Well, I don't think I'm going to be prejudiced," I answered.

A gentle smile cracked her mouth as she said, "That's nice."

Over time, however, paying attention to what I was hearing about race didn't give me a good feeling, especially about the black folks in Cape. They had so much to say about the evils of the white man, but nothing about their own shortcomings or their place in the world. There seemed to be only a few destinies for black men in Cape Girardeau, such as a career in the military or on the back of a garbage truck. And so many spent time in jail that I came to think of it as a rite of passage. But rather than demanding better opportunities, they seemed to accept inequity and disparate treatment.

In later years, I would learn more about the history of race in America, and I gained a greater appreciation for the complex reasons why oppressed people in the United States struggle to make the same gains as white Americans. But based on my childhood impression of Cape's black folks, I grew to despise them.

>‹‹

OVER TIME, I became increasingly confused about what I was supposed to feel about myself and where I was supposed to fit in. I obviously wasn't white. But judging by the attitudes and behaviors of the black people around me, I wasn't black, either.

Making matters worse, I was constantly being chastised for the un-blackness of my behavior by my brothers and by most every other black person in Cape.

"Jeff, you walk funny. Why do you walk like that?"

"Jeff, why don't you finish the meat on that chicken bone? Look at that, boy done left all that food on the bone."

"Don't you know how to sweep the floor? You doin' it like white folks."

"Why you use all them fancy words when you talk? You talk like white folks. Who you trying to impress?"

Maybe my family and friends meant nothing more than gentle teasing. But I took their comments to heart, especially since there was no one around to console me. It was up to me alone to figure out how to be black enough to be accepted by my family and community. I used to spend hours in my backyard trying to develop that hip in my walk that my brothers and everyone else in the neighborhood had. I used to sneak up to my brothers' rooms and try on their platform shoes; I couldn't wait to be old enough to have my own pair, which I figured would surely prove my credentials as a black man. I can't tell you the distress I felt when platforms went out of style.

One of the biggest nonblack characteristics about me was my hair. "Jeff, what's wrong with yo' 'fro?" came from everyone. It seemed my hair was extra kinky and always nappy. During my youth, the afro style was just starting to lose steam, and since it was long before the natural, nappy-headed look became hip, I was having nothing but bad hair days. The problem became apparent one day in grade school. I had my head down doing some reading at my desk when a classmate sneaked up behind me and started to pick my hair. In shock, I turned around and saw the rest of the class encouraging the activity and laughing at me. All I could do was sit there and cry. After that day, I wore a hat everywhere I went.

For years afterward, trying my best to fit in, I would awaken for school much earlier than necessary and spend a long time in front of the bathroom mirror trying to get my hair in an acceptable shape. Getting a haircut was always a drama, since I never wanted to take my hat off. "Mr. Bond" was a bald, middle-aged man who made house calls to cut hair. I always ran away when I saw his car parked in front of the house, but my brothers would find me and drag me back, kicking and screaming all the way. As my hair rolled down the apron while Mr. Bond snipped away, I felt part of me was being cut off.

Later, when most of the black guys in town started getting their hair braided, I decided to follow suit. I asked "Amina," the neighborhood braid girl, to do mine after she finished my brother's. As she yanked, pulled, and twisted my hair, I felt as if it was being torn up by the roots. "You must be tender headed," Amina remarked. Once the French braids she made were finished, I didn't wear the hat as much— because, although I thought I looked ridiculous with the rows of braids in my hair, I definitely felt blacker.

I tried everything I could think of to measure up to other people's concept of blackness. I hung out with those I considered blacker than me, but somehow their blackness never rubbed off on me. It got so bad that I started to suspect that anything I heard from the black people around me was part of a black code I wasn't privy to. For example, I heard people using the term "Mother's Day" for the first of every month, in sentences like, "Well, it's Mother's Day again, they gonna be out on the streets tonight." I had no idea what it meant. Only years later did I discover that the first of the month was when the young mothers received their assistance checks from the government. When I discovered the meaning, I once again felt not black enough to get it.

Religion was a problem for me as well. I grew up assuming that all black folks believed in God and were duty bound to attend church every Sunday. I heard comments like "Have faith in Jesus," "Read the Bible," and "Thank the Lord" everywhere I turned, even from people who seemed to have no serious interest in religion. I couldn't share these easy consolations. In fact, I had nothing but questions about religion: "Why are all the pictures of Jesus in church white? How can there be a Devil or Hell if God is all-powerful? Did King James, or whoever wrote the Bible, really have black people in mind?" But whenever I tried to ask my mother for answers to these questions, the conversation quickly ended with her admonishing me to pray more often.

Over time, my skepticism only grew. I felt that if you've seen one black preacher, you've seen them all. The look is always the same—heavyset, with the typical "preacher roll" at the back of the neck—and so is the sound: a deep, raspy voice that makes a grunted "hah" at the end of every phrase (there must be a school of some kind where that "hah" is taught to black preachers). The preacher was always the most highly respected person in the community, but to me he was just another man.

Religion was so deeply rooted in the black community in Cape that my skepticism caused me to have doubts about my own blackness. Could it be that I was not black enough for God?

My attitude toward learning was yet another way I felt alienated from the people around me. For most black people in Cape Girardeau, education seemed to be an afterthought, a nuisance to get through with no real purpose. You might think that doing well in school would

be a source of pride, but in my community good grades were an indication of difference, arrogance, or, worst of all, aspiring to be white.

It wasn't always that way. Most of the elders in Cape had high
school diplomas, including my grandmother and all five of her sisters,
my mother and her brother, and most of their friends. In fact, many, including my mother, had taken at least a course or two in college. What
I found astounding was that they'd all gone to school in the days when
there was legal school segregation in Cape. They'd attended John S.
Cobb School, the black school, rather than Cape Central, which was
the white school. I enjoyed hearing stories about the struggle for education that blacks went through in Cape during the John S. Cobb
reunions, which my mother had helped to organize.

"The only books we got were the used ones from Central, and they
would be in horrible condition when they would send them over."

"Because we had the leftover books, our subjects were limited, but
we had teachers that gave a damn and taught us right."

My mother graduated in the top five of her class and recounted her
attempts to go further: "The year was 1952, and a local pastor took the
five of us up to the local university to register. We were turned away
that day. Integration didn't come along until 1954." She eventually
took some classes at Southern Illinois University, which was across the
river and a good ways from home.

Somewhere along the way, the value of education seemed to have
been lost on most of the black people of Cape. I couldn't understand why. Not only did my mother provide the example of the value
of getting an education for me, but so did the earlier generations
in Cape like my grandmother and great aunts and uncles, who all
achieved at least a high school diploma. To them, despite the unfair
disparity between white and black schools, they saw the value and
not the color of education. Things had apparently changed greatly,
to my dismay, over the years, and school took on the province of
white and not embraced as the generations before demonstrated. Because enjoying school was viewed as being white, I couldn't share my
love of learning with anyone else.

In the fifth grade, I fell in love with the music of KC and the Sunshine Band, especially their horn section. I decided I wanted to learn how to play the saxophone. So one day when I saw a flyer at school offering music lessons, I jumped at the opportunity. My mother reluctantly paid for a used alto sax at a local store. Every day I was dismissed from class for a couple of hours to take lessons with a white saxophone instructor who would pick me up from school. I was excited to be learning something new and fun, despite the smirks from my classmates.

It was difficult at home as well. When I tried to practice, my mother would yell, "Goddamn it, Jeff! Stop that! Can't you do that some other time? I can't hear the TV." I ended up trying to get to school early or stay late in order to practice. My mother occasionally attended my concerts, but she mostly treated my music as merely a showpiece for her friends. At times, I had to conceal my tears while obeying her command to play something, knowing my music really meant nothing to her personally.

It was the same with my schoolwork. Talk about school never extended beyond the canned exchange, "So, Jeff, what did you learn in school today?" "Not much." Because of the constant commotion in our house, I had to do my best to finish my homework before I left school.

Once I got to high school, I took advanced placement courses and usually got excellent grades. Soon enough, I was the only black kid in most of my classes. Only on the school bus and in the cafeteria did I mingle with the black students, who gave me endless grief for taking those "white-kid classes." They also thought it strange that I didn't go to summer school, which most black kids had to do to make up for their failures during the school year. It all went to reaffirm their view of me as an Oreo—black on the outside, white on the inside.

The white people didn't know what to make of me either. I had one English teacher who never called on me, even when I was the only one in the class to raise my hand. When she gave me a midterm grade of D, rather than an A or B as I normally earned, the guidance counselor called me into his office. "Are you having problems at home, Jeffrey?" he asked.

I was reluctant to blame my low grade on someone else, but I eventually told the counselor, "I don't think the teacher likes black people." He brushed that aside, insisting the problem must be in my home. I realized that if I was going to learn anything in that class or anywhere else, I'd have to do it on my own. Eventually, through sheer determination, I got an A minus in the class.

Realizing that, for all my efforts, I couldn't satisfy the expectations of either the black people I lived among or the white people who barely recognized my existence, I finally stopped trying. Since neither the black world nor the white world wanted me, I decided to belong to neither. I decided to be Jeffrey who is proud to be black without being defined by his color—as if I could live in an America beyond race, like the one I learned about in books and on television.

It was a lonely life, since no one I knew was prepared to see me as the unique, post-racial person that I aspired to be. It was during this time that I began having a recurring nightmare, a dream that would return to haunt my sleep in later years whenever life was throwing tough obstacles in my way.

The dream was always the same: I am tiny, like the character played by Grant Williams in one of my favorite 1950s sci-fi movies, *The Incredible Shrinking Man*. Everything is dark, and I'm dwarfed by the overwhelming size of everything I see or sense around me. Unlike in the movie, I'm not being hunted by a huge cat or giant insects, but there seems to be an unseen specter after me as I am trying to traverse an impossible, larger-than-life dreamscape. Just when I feel the journey is about to reach some horrible end, I find that I have stopped fleeing. Now I am alone in a dark room with no windows, doors, lights, or sounds.

Suddenly I see myself—only it is an older version of me, curled up with his head resting on his knees, crying as if to express a feeling of absolute hopelessness. Then that me looks up. I see a wrinkled, worn-out face, streaming with tears. I can see in that face an unspoken plea: *Just give up. It is all too hard. There is no way out.*

At this moment, just as I turn to run, I awaken from the nightmare, trembling and in a cold sweat.

This dream has returned to me periodically throughout my life, more intense and more real than any other. I'm sure it has reflected some of the fundamental realities of my life, especially the increasing difficulty I faced in trying to avoid choosing a color and a restricted place for myself in a deeply divided America.

Despair was an option that continually tempted me. Yet I was determined to continue the quest to be who I wanted to be, on my terms, although I didn't know then the price I would ultimately pay.

# CHAPTER THREE

# The Escape

I N 1985, WHEN MY SENIOR YEAR OF HIGH SCHOOL CAME AROUND, there was never a question in my mind as to whether I was going to go to college. I don't know where the motivation came from, but I couldn't imagine any other path to take in life.

Cape is home to Southeast Missouri State University, but SEMO was a completely foreign world to me and to everyone I knew in Cape. The blacks that attended SEMO came from southern states like Georgia, Mississippi, and Alabama and were referred to as "them up there at SEMO," as if they were a breed apart from the regular blacks of Cape.

When the time came to apply, I didn't know where I wanted to go to college. I only knew that I didn't want to stay in Cape. My stubbornness made for quite the session with my high school guidance counselor.

"Jeff, have you thought about what major you want up at SEMO?" the counselor asked.

"I'm not going to SEMO," I responded.

"SEMO is a good school, and I think you'll have a great opportunity to do well there," he said, sounding a bit confused.

"That may be so, but I'm not going to SEMO. I want to go somewhere else, and I'll get back to you when I figure out where I want to go."

I researched a number of schools, but I felt like I was shooting in the dark until one of my mother's friends, who was a prominent lawyer in Cape, called me into his office for a chat. His name was "Garry," and he was a tallish man with salt-and-pepper hair and wire-rimmed glasses. He reminded me of the sort of father figure one would see in those old Norman Rockwell paintings, except, of course, that he was a black man.

"Have you ever heard of Millikin University?" he asked me.

"No, can't say that I have," I replied, trying to sound confident.

"It's a fine institution in Decatur, Illinois. My wife and I both went there," Garry explained. I was captivated by his description. It was the first and only time that anyone had ever talked to me about college options, and by the time I walked out of his office I knew that I was going to go to Millikin University.

Now that I had found a school, money was going to be a factor. I gathered the forms for institutional and federal loans, and I was trying to fill them out when I came to parts that required my mother's signature. It was a weekday evening, and Miss Helen was entertaining a friend in the living room. I had asked her to take a look at the forms a couple of weeks earlier, but for some reason she hadn't. The deadline was fast approaching, and I needed her attention.

"Mother, I need you for just one second," I interjected calmly as she was talking to her friend. "Could you please come and take a look at these forms?"

"Not now, Jeff. Can't you see we have company?" Her tone was sharp and angry.

I felt anger well up inside me like never before. Then it exploded. "I never ask you for anything. But I need you right now, for just a few moments. Is talking to your friend over beer more important than helping your son go to college?!" The loan forms were slightly crumpled in my hand, which was becoming a clenched fist.

Miss Helen and her friend looked shocked. It was the first time I'd ever raised my voice to her. Without asking a single question, she signed where I indicated.

I knew I had to look for other resources. I decided to call the United Negro College Fund, having seen their TV commercials a thousand times. I was nervous as I dialed the 800 number.

"Hi. I was wondering if you could give me some information about the United Negro College Fund and how I go about applying for assistance in going to college," I asked.

"What school are you going to?" the operator asked.

"I've been accepted to Millikin University," I said proudly.

"I've never heard of that school. Is it predominantly black?" she asked.

"What does that have to do with anything?"

"In order to receive assistance from the United Negro College Fund, you have to go to a predominantly black school."

As I had discovered on a visit to Millikin, the school was predominantly white. "Wait a minute! You mean to tell me that even though I am black, I can't have access to your assistance unless I go to a black school?"

"That's right."

"But there's no black school anywhere near me."

"I'm sorry, but feel free to give us a call back when you decide to attend a black school." It sounded as if the operator was condemning me for my decision.

For a moment, my heart sank. Then I was flooded with anger. "Why am I limited in where I want to go just because I'm black?" I was pissed off at everything I'd grown up with. Once again, I felt I was being condemned for not being black enough.

To get through college, I ended up taking out every loan I could find. I also took a job on campus as a political science tutor. My mother assisted me when she could, but her help amounted to almost nothing. I found that I was proud to be paying my own way, without relying on any race-based support.

My freshman year at Millikin was the first time I'd been away from home, and I was scared to death. The first new experience was my roommate, "Matt." He was from rural Illinois, and I don't think he'd ever seen a black person in his life until that first day when I walked into the room. About the middle of the first semester, Matt confessed his feelings at meeting me.

"You know, I was a bit afraid to have a black roommate," he said with a trembling voice. "Not that I thought you would be . . . well, you know what I mean."

"Yeah, sure. No problem."

"Just like there are people that can be considered white trash. There are, you know, blacks that can be considered, uh, you know, niggers. And, uh, not that I thought you were a, uh, nigger."

"Well, I know some find it easy to use that word to categorize people. But I would prefer that you not use that word in my presence again. I mean, I would never refer to anyone as white trash. That's just the type of person I am."

Matt nodded. "And you know something?" he asked with a calmer voice. "You don't really look like I expected. Your nose is smaller than I thought it would be."

Not really knowing how to respond, I said, "Really? Well, I guess us black folks have all different kinds of features, just like you white folks."

We both had a good laugh at that.

I found it easy to make friends on campus. I was amazed at how many of the white students, most of them from the Midwest, had never seen any black people before coming to Millikin. What I took comfort in was the fact that I didn't feel as alien with them as I did with the white people in Cape. No one completely disregarded color; it just didn't seem to be the defining factor in our relationship.

The black students were another story. Most of them came from cities like Chicago, Milwaukee, and Cincinnati, and they had a swagger about them that was completely unfamiliar to me. None of them had ever heard of Cape Girardeau, so they viewed me as a sort of country boy.

Several of us were having lunch one day at one of the black tables in the cafeteria. "We're trying to organize a step show. Jeff, have you ever been to a step show?" I was asked by one of the black leaders on campus.

I couldn't hide my ignorance, "A step show? What's that?"

Collectively, the table sighed. "You've never heard of a step show?" someone remarked. "Damn, you *are* country!"

I tried to laugh off my embarrassment as they explained to me that a step show is a dance competition among black fraternities, each doing their own "steps." I could stand their teasing, since I was used to it from back home, but I hated their constant use of the word "nigger." Over and over I heard, "Niggah please!" "That nigger is crazy." "Nigger this" and "nigger that." I was shocked. This was college, not Cape Girardeau. I'd found myself looking up to these city blacks, but now they reminded me of the place I'd escaped from. I was very confused.

In order to get the full effect of college, I wanted the social experience of being in a fraternity. There were five fraternities at Millikin. The traditionally black fraternity was Alpha Phi Alpha. The primary difference between it and the white fraternities was that the A-Phis didn't have a house of their own, which was understandable because their membership numbered only around five or six. During my first semester at Millikin, I decided to join A-Phi-A.

However, the more time I spent with the A-Phis, the more I realized I was in the wrong place. Having escaped Cape, I was back in a separatist environment, shut off from the rest of the campus and involved with people who preferred not to socialize with the nonblack students. I felt I was bowing to pressure to stay black at all costs—even though the pressure may have only been in my mind.

I decided to switch to Tau Kappa Epsilon, a traditionally white fraternity that most of my white friends had joined. The Eureka College branch of TKE had once boasted Ronald Reagan as a member, and for a time I was the only black member at Millikin. But I didn't see my action as a social statement, because I was simply doing what I wanted. In joining TKE, I wasn't saying no to the black students—I was finally saying yes to my own interests.

Another new sensation was having an academic mentor who seemed to genuinely care about my interests and my progress. Dr. Robert McIntire, head of the political science department, was a Mel Tormé look-alike with the addition of rather scholarly glasses. McIntire was a brilliant man, and I took every opportunity to take his classes. More important, he seemed to believe in me and took more notice of my potential than anyone else had done.

All in all, I felt excited and happy to have escaped from Cape, and to have found a place where I could grow into something bigger and better. But my escape wasn't complete. I realized that during my summer vacation in 1987, when I returned to Cape after my sophomore year at Millikin.

⊰⊱

IT WAS A typical July day in Cape. The air was steamy and the sun unrelenting. Mother had left for work an hour or so before, and I was in the kitchen reading the local newspaper. I glanced up and noticed my mother's car pulling into the backyard. This was odd. It wasn't lunchtime yet, and I had rarely seen her park in the backyard. She had a haggard look on her face as she approached the house.

She entered the kitchen through the back door, walked directly to the refrigerator, got a beer, and slumped down in a chair at the kitchen table. There was an uncomfortable silence.

"Mother," I said, "what's wrong?"

"Mind your own business," she replied, glaring at me.

I left the room, figuring that she might decide to talk with me later.

Time passed, and several people came to visit my mother, including a coworker. I was two rooms away, and I could overhear a bit of their talking. "Are you all right, Miss Helen?" was the main question they asked. Then I heard my mother say something that gave me an awful chill: "I should just kill myself and get it all over with."

I walked back into the kitchen. "Mother," I asked, "what's wrong? Why would you say something like that?"

"Don't you worry about it. I told you to mind your own business."

Suddenly I found myself exploding.

"I've never asked you for anything!" I shouted, my fists clenched and trembling. Once again, I was asking something of my mother, and once again I felt the need to remind her what type of son I had been to her. "I have always been here for you, and now I'm asking you what's wrong and you won't tell me a thing! You have no problem talking to everyone else, but you tell me to mind my own business."

She looked up at me in silence. After a moment, I left the kitchen and ran upstairs to an empty bedroom, sweltering in the summer heat. I started to cry uncontrollably.

After a couple of hours, I went back downstairs. I heard my mother laughing with her guests in the kitchen. The phone was off the hook, and all the doors, normally wide open, were closed. I looked out the front door and there was a news crew from the local television station parked outside. The day continued in an eerie sort of quiet, interrupted only by her conversations with guests who dropped by to speak with her. It felt as if there'd been a terrible tragedy that everyone knew about—except me.

Around 5 p.m., everyone who was in the house gathered to watch the early evening news. Having nothing else to do, I joined them in the living room. I never had much interest in the local news programming, but this broadcast hit me like a ton of bricks. I can't re-create the precise wording of the news story, but the anchorman's report went something like this:

Our top story this evening: Longtime clerk of the municipal court Helen Sterling was fired today after an extensive internal investigation at the police department uncovered improprieties related to revenues collected at the station from court costs and traffic tickets. Spokesmen for the police station said that, over a number of years, the coffers at the station had been coming up short, and that Miss

Sterling was the lead suspect, as she was in charge of collecting the funds from citizens paying parking or traffic-related fines, including court costs. Miss Sterling stands accused of embezzling upward of sixty thousand dollars from the department. Miss Sterling was unavailable for comment.

I looked over at my mother. She almost seemed to glow from the attention given to her by the program and her friends. I walked out of the house and down to the river. I sat there for hours gazing over the water, much the way I did as a child.

For a few days, I clung to the belief that there had to be a terrible mistake. My mother wouldn't, couldn't, do such a thing.

Then she confessed to all the charges.

Later that horrible summer, and as the sentencing date neared, my mother and her family members were summoned to her attorney's office for a strategy session. To elicit sympathy from the judge, the attorney planned to call character witnesses from the community as well as "the boys" to speak on behalf of Miss Helen.

"We want to make sure she doesn't get a prison sentence," the attorney said. "Chances are the judge will suspend the sentence and require her to pay back some of the money. The job then will be to make sure she's able to pay it back. She'll need help from all of you."

His words reinforced a decision I'd made soon after my mother's confession. I would stay in Cape to help her in any way that I could. Later that evening, I had a conversation with her about it.

"Mother, I'm not going to go back to school this fall," I said. "You are going to need help here."

"No, Jeff, you go back to school," she said. "I'll be all right, don't worry about me. I'll be fine."

"We'll see," I said. And with that, the only conversation we had since the ordeal began was over.

Sentencing took place on another brutally hot day. The courtroom was filled with friends and family, well-wishers and curiosity-seekers. My brothers and I sat along with other relatives in the pews directly behind the defendant's table where my mother sat. I had spent many hours in that very courtroom watching my mother working as the court clerk. Now she was here as a convicted felon.

My mother's attorney called a string of witnesses who vouched for her character and her big heart. There were stories of how she looked in on elderly citizens, how she never turned anyone away from her home, and how she was a mother figure to so many people in Cape.

Then came my turn to speak. Most of the people there only knew me as Miss Helen's youngest son and not much else. But as I approached the stand, I could sense every eye in the place focusing on me, and it gave me a strange, chilling sensation. After preliminary questions, the attorney came to the main questions he wanted to ask.

"You are in college right now, is that correct?"

"Yes I am. I just finished my sophomore year."

"How are you paying for your expenses?"

"I take out student loans and I have a job on campus," I said.

The prosecutor then rose to cross-examine. "How much money would you say your mother has given you to attend college?"

"During my time in college, she has maybe given me a couple of hundred dollars or so," I explained. "As I said, most of my expenses are covered by loans and my campus job."

Almost cutting me off, he blurted, "No more questions, your honor."

I glanced over at my mother, but she didn't look back. When I left the stand, I caressed her shoulder as I passed her to take my seat. Still, she didn't look up at me.

Then the prosecutor began presenting the arguments that he believed would justify a stiff sentence for Miss Helen. He said he would show cause as to why my mother would embezzle such a large sum of money. There had been wide speculation in town that she could not have been solely responsible for the substantial sum missing from the coffers, and it was his job to eliminate any such doubt so that there would be no hesitation about bringing the full force of the law down upon her.

His first witness was a police officer, dressed neatly in his uniform. The initial questions concerned procedures at the police station, including how my mother was responsible for collecting the fines and turning in the monies to the officer in charge at the end of the day. The last question to the officer caught my attention.

"Do you have any idea as to why she would have embezzled such a substantial sum of money?" the prosecutor asked.

"I don't really know," said the officer. "I do know that she has a son going to college, Harvard or somewhere like that. I know college is pretty expensive."

Everything suddenly became very clear to me. Everyone, including the officer and maybe even the prosecutor, believed that my mother had taken the money to fund my college education. She never took the stand, so there was never any opportunity to counter the belief that I was at fault for her criminal action, and she never so much as said a word to the contrary to me.

At the end of the hearing, the judge sentenced my mother to probation and ordered her to pay $40,000 in restitution. I felt as if the judge were sentencing me.

That evening, sitting alone by the river, I made the toughest decision I'd ever made. I decided to return to college. There was nothing for me in Cape any longer.

I returned to Millikin earlier than usual. I couldn't bear to tell anyone about the summer I had experienced. Not a day passed when I didn't feel a tinge of guilt for being away when Miss Helen was going through so much. I continually agonized over the same questions: Did I make the right decision? What kind of son am I? Was there really anything I could do? And I had to reassure myself over and over again that Miss Helen hadn't done what she did because of me.

The only counter to the shame I felt was my anger over having to make the decision to leave. That anger became the fuel I needed to continue on the course I had set for myself. Now that I no longer had a mother or family, all I could do was to throw myself into learning and thinking about my future. I immersed myself in my studies, and I reached out more than ever to my professors for advice and guidance, particularly Dr. McIntire.

The school year passed by without much contact between me and the folks in Cape. I would call occasionally to speak with Miss Helen, and she never seemed in bad spirits or troubled in any way. It was difficult talking with her. I was trying to figure out who she had become and why I hadn't seen it coming. The phone conversations were always the same.

"Hi," I would say without emotion.

"Hi," she would respond.

"How's everything?"

"Everything is fine. I'm all right. How is school?"

"It's okay." A brief silence. "Well, I'm glad everything's okay. I'll talk to you later."

"Okay. Love you."

"Yeah." I could not bring myself to return the sentiment.

Though I didn't travel home for the traditional holidays like Easter and Thanksgiving, I felt obliged to spend the summer in Cape. When I arrived, I noticed people looking at me in a new way, particularly my brothers. It felt as if they wanted to put me on trial to accept responsibility for the fall that Miss Helen had taken. I was the pariah, and Miss Helen had nothing to say in my defense. In fact, we rarely spoke to each other. She was no longer my mother; I didn't know who she was. Her appearance, mannerisms, everything seemed different. She no longer put much effort into her looks: her clothes and hair seemed perpetually disheveled, and her face bore a bitterness I had not seen before. She was also drinking more. What was particularly striking to me was the way she talked. She had begun to curse and was accentuating her speech with formerly forbidden phrases like "you know" and "ain't."

One day, I had to butt in to a conversation she was having with a friend on the front porch. "That niggah ain't no good," I heard my mother say.

"Excuse me," I said, "but I can remember a time when you told me not to use words like 'you know,' 'ain't,' and especially 'nigger.'"

"I never said no such thing! That's just the way people talk. Ain't nothing wrong with it. They may not talk that way up in that college of yours, but that's the way we talk here." It was apparent she had a point to make, as she continued, "I know you don't like black folks anyway."

"What do you mean by that?" I asked.

"Well, Millikin is all white, right?" She placed emphasis on "all white" for the benefit of her guest. "And you never really seemed to like the black folks around here anyway."

"What does that have to do with anything?" I asked.

"Oh, nothing. I just thought you decided to go there because you don't like black people." And with that, she dismissed me and returned to her company.

Who was this woman?

There was another incident that summer that further solidified the estrangement. One day I retrieved the mail and noticed catalogs for women's clothing from stores like Lane Bryant and August Max addressed to me. At first I thought it was just a mistake. But something didn't feel right. I decided to do a bit of investigating.

There was a particular side of the living room couch where Miss Helen usually sat. I remembered that she would sometimes put letters under the cushion on that side, especially if it was something she didn't want anyone else to see. The next time she went out, I took a look. Under the cushion, I found several statements from the same companies whose catalogs I'd found in the mail. All of them had balances well into the hundreds of dollars, and they all had my name as debtor.

When Miss Helen returned with my older brother, I confronted her with the evidence.

"What's this? Why do these bills have my name on them?" I asked as calmly as I could. There was hesitation before she answered.

"Oh, I needed some clothes, so I took out a few accounts in your name," she said confidently.

"How were you able to do that? And why would you do such a thing?"

"I *am* your mother, and I know your social security number," she replied. "I did it to help you get good credit. You're going to need a good credit rating, ya know!"

My brother agreed. "Her taking out those accounts will help you have good credit," he said in a fatherly fashion. "Don't worry about it."

I stood there stunned. My fists clenched around the bills and catalogs. Their reasoning was completely ridiculous, and I was growing angry.

"Well, I'm not going to have good credit if you don't pay these bills. And how many more are there that I haven't seen?"

"Those look like the only ones. I'm doing this to help you!" my mother said.

"Look, she needed something, and you should be glad to help out in this way," my older brother chimed in. There was silence as they both stared at me, as if daring me to ask anything else. I wanted to press the issue further, but I was outnumbered, and they were doing a good job of pushing the guilt button.

I returned to school feeling even more deeply alienated from my family.

One day the following January, my phone rang. "Mr. Sterling?" said a rather official-sounding voice. He explained that he was from a collection agency and that the purpose of the call was an attempt to collect a debt. It turned out that several of the accounts Miss Helen had taken out in my name were long delinquent and in collection. From the conversation, I gathered that nothing had ever been paid on any of the accounts.

As soon as I hung up, I called home.

"Hello, can I speak to Miss Helen, please?" I asked, having no idea who had answered the phone.

After a long silence, the person who'd answered the call said, "She's not here."

"When will she be back?"

"I don't know. She's in jail."

Evidently, my mother wasn't living up to the court's restitution requirements as prescribed, so they'd locked her up to provide some motivation. I had to wait another week before I finally spoke with her. In the meantime, I received calls from two other collection agencies, both identical to the initial call.

When I did finally speak with her, her reply was almost accusatory. "Look, I'm sorry. I'll take care of it. Don't worry about it, okay?"

"All right," I said. I hung up, knowing that things would only get worse.

Over the next month, the calls from the collection agencies continued. Nothing had been paid, and Miss Helen hadn't talked to them as she'd promised. I had no choice but to call the collection agencies and explain the situation honestly. Soon after, the calls and notices stopped.

I never discussed the matter with my mother again. I didn't feel as if there was anything left for us to talk about.

# CHAPTER FOUR

# In Search of America

DㅤURING MY SENIOR YEAR AT MILLIKIN, I FELL IN LOVE FOR the first time. Her name was "Sandy," and she was a freshman—and white. At first, I didn't know how to be a boyfriend. As a kid in Cape, I'd been mocked as being "afraid of girls," and some people even intimated that I might be gay. So I was surprised to find that I liked the whole relationship thing, and our differences in age and in color posed no apparent obstacle. I became increasingly comfortable with Sandy as we spent time together and grew closer.

No one from my family had ever bothered to visit me during my years at college, but many of them turned out for my graduation. I was proud of what I had accomplished, and I was elated to share it with them—until I watched Miss Helen emerge from a sheriff's van on that bright May day in handcuffs. I spent that night crying in Sandy's arms rather than celebrating.

Luckily, I did not have the time for any prolonged lamentation. I was busy getting ready to attend Washington University School of Law, in St. Louis, in the fall. I had been accepted to four other schools, but finances had narrowed my options to Washington, which was the closest to home. Everything was fine until the financial aid rejections started to arrive. I'd been flagged as a bad credit risk thanks to the "good credit" Miss Helen had helped me obtain. Out of necessity, I became an expert on credit. It took numerous phone calls and letters to every credit reporting agency, but I finally got the mess cleared up and secured the necessary loans.

I felt a little nervous about going to law school, especially without family support. My brothers dismissed my concerns and belittled my aspirations, saying things like, "I could have gone to college and law school, too—I just didn't want to." Even worse was my grandmother's comment: "I think it was okay that you went to college, but law school . . . " she said. "I think that's beyond where black folks should be."

"Well, I think I'll be all right" was all I could say.

Sandy dropped out of Millikin and decided to accompany me to St. Louis, and my family's reaction to her reinforced my sense of estrangement. One evening after Sandy and I had spent the day with my family, my brother John confronted me. "She's nice and all," he said, "but you're not going to marry her, are you? I mean, you can't be marrying a white girl."

"What business is it of yours if I do?" I responded coldly.

I was done trying to please them. I would continue to visit home from time to time, and to communicate with my mother and my brothers. But I would no longer allow their attitudes to influence my thoughts or actions. This was my life, and I was going to live it the way I wanted.

Sandy and I found an apartment in St. Louis and settled in. We adopted a couple of tiny kittens that had been left in a box behind the local Walmart. I named them Pee Wee and Marble, and they became cherished friends of mine for years to come. It was nice finally living in a city, with its constant motion, sounds, and excitement. Sandy and I didn't have much money, but we made our way. Law school felt like a natural continuation of college. I put as much effort into studying there as I did at Millikin. And, much like at Millikin, I found myself in contact with a teacher who had quite an impact on me.

Languishing in the required first-year courses, I had the opportunity to take a contracts class with a professor by the name of A. Peter Mutharika. He was from Malawi and had a thick accent that some students found difficult to follow, coupled with a commanding, even intimidating presence. During the legal case analysis portions of his lectures, you could sense the collective "please don't call on me" vibe from the other students. Professor Mutharika was the first black male teacher I had ever had, and I was captivated by him. I took every opportunity to meet with him and get his insights into the legal profession and life in general. The fact that he was a successful black man provided a level of inspiration that I deeply appreciated. Years later, in 2014, Mutharika became president of Malawi, a post he still holds in 2019.

Unlike my early days at college, I didn't feel any pressure to stick with my own kind on the law school campus. There was more of a professional feeling among the students, and I liked it. I joined the Black Law Students Association and found it a comfortable, congenial setting.

I was also maturing, especially with regard to race issues. At times, I found it painful to learn about the legal history of blacks in this country. But it was also encouraging to see how black Americans had persevered and fought for the rights they deserved. It was all right there in those heavy law books, and I was absolutely fascinated by it. The new things I was learning helped me to finally put into words some of the feelings about race that I'd been unable to understand or convey.

My new perspective on race was reflected in a conversation I had with a fellow black student one day. His name was "Desmond," and he was an affable and confident student with a bit of a revolutionary streak about him. He had recently attended a seminar on black empowerment and had come to believe that the only answer to the nation's racial troubles was a complete separation of the races.

"You know," he told me, "if you look at the letters in America, they spell 'I Am Race.'"

After a bit of a silence, I had to ask, "And that means . . . what?"

"It means that even the name of this country is completely de-fined by race." As if mounting a soapbox, Desmond continued, "And because of this, we as a people will never have the same rights as the white man. In this country, the black race will always be at the bottom of the racial pool."

I felt I had to push back. "But if we refrain from allowing ourselves to be defined by the color of our skin," I said, "if we refuse to fall into the stereotypical norms that have been developed over the years, then won't such a racial system naturally collapse? I'm not saying that we have to reject matters of black or African culture. All I'm saying is that we don't have to be defined by it." I was on the soapbox now. "You can rearrange letters all you want, but this is still America, and we should be able to be and do anything we want regardless of our race."

"Well, Jeff, that's a good way to look at it," Desmond said. "Let's hope that it really comes to that someday."

It was not so easy for me to make optimistic statements about race walking the streets of St. Louis with Sandy. The stares and whispers were obvious. One of the rare times when I felt driven to react hap-pened in the U-City Loop, an area of St. Louis with trendy bars and restaurants catering to a college crowd. We passed a couple of young black women on the sidewalk, and when I heard them making some snide comments, I turned to look. They had stopped in the middle of the sidewalk and were staring at Sandy and me as if we were on display.

I couldn't let this pass. I grabbed Sandy in a warm embrace and said to the two gawkers, "You wanna see something? Here, look at this!" I proceeded to plant a big wet one on Sandy's lips.

Their jaws dropped, and one shouted with amazement, "And it's his wife!" The fact that she used the word "it" to refer to Sandy made my disgust and anger even stronger.

I first met Sandy's family while I was still in college. I think I struck them as a bit of a mystery, or at least not what they expected in a black man. As we sat down to our first dinner in their home, I think Sandy's stepmother was more anxious than I was.

"Now Jeff," she said apologetically, "we're not formal around here. You just get what you want from the kitchen and have a seat."

To hide my own nervousness, I laughed and said, "That's exactly the way we used to eat at my house, so this is perfect to me." She seemed relieved at my response, and we got along well from that moment on.

Only after Sandy and I moved in together in St. Louis did her family express any concern over our relationship. One evening, her father took me aside and quietly told me, "I don't have a problem with your relationship. I'm just concerned about the trouble you might have from other people, especially the tough time your kids might have."

I can't say I was surprised at his statement, but I was glad he made it. It is always so much easier to sidestep issues of race than to confront them head on. I responded the only way I knew how. "I think we'll be okay. And when it comes to kids, my feeling is that, as long as Sandy and I love our children as much as we can, what other people think or say just won't matter."

I was speaking from the heart, expressing my deepest conviction not just about the kids that Sandy and I might have someday but about the quest for personal freedom and acceptance that was at the very center of my life. I don't know whether I convinced Sandy's dad or not, but he appeared satisfied with my response. I was pleased he was okay with Sandy and me, and in time he became more like a father to me than my own.

My years at law school passed by quickly. As I entered the last semester, I hadn't had much success in lining up a job at a law firm, but I was still hopeful. One day I came across a newspaper want ad that caught my eye. Next to a drawing of a stealthy-looking man peering out over a canal was the headline, "Serve your country and see the world in a unique opportunity." Those words captured my imagination. I read on, and discovered that the ad was for operational officer positions with the Central Intelligence Agency.

I was hooked. I knew nothing about the CIA other than its mystique, but I wanted to get out and see the world that I had fantasized about for most of my life. I also noticed the bold sentence at the bottom of the ad noting that the "CIA is an equal opportunity employer."

I discussed the matter with Sandy and decided to apply. Over the next few months, I went through a number of interviews with CIA officials, all without knowing how long the process would take. I received background materials that explained the mission of the Agency and offered some idea of what it would be like to work there. One of the points made was that the CIA strove for diversity in its workforce, which made sense to me—after all, the CIA should resemble the world it's charged with keeping an eye on. I liked the idea of being part of an organization where I would be judged for myself rather than viewed through racial stereotypes.

On the other hand, there were certain things about the interviews that concerned me. For example, in each interview, I was asked why I hadn't turned out like other members of my family—plagued by various life problems and circumstances. The only reason I could come up with was, "I didn't want that." But the implication that I might be somehow tainted by the shortcomings of my family members made me uneasy. This gave me something to worry about as the prolonged application process continued.

Law school graduation arrived. Sandy and I entertained members of my family at our apartment. My mother was among then, having finally finished serving out her prison term. My family's presence didn't mean much to me—I felt great about what I'd achieved, but my sense of disconnection from them was stronger than ever. The most memorable moment came when my oldest brother's girlfriend asked me, "Jeff, where did you get the inspiration to succeed like you have?" I silently gestured toward Miss Helen. My mother beamed at the suggestion that she was the inspiration for my achievements. It might have broken her heart to know my real meaning—that I'd been inspired to *not* be like her. Thinking about it broke my heart a little too.

Now that I'd graduated, the pressure was really on to find a job. I was still hopeful about a position with the CIA, but in the meantime, I applied for a job with the St. Louis Public Defender's office. This was the kind of work that many young black attorneys gravitated toward, and I didn't like the idea of being stuck in a position that could reinforce the stereotyped views others might have of me. At least I would get some practical legal experience.

As I hadn't yet taken the Missouri bar, I was hired as a legal assistant until I could take the test. It was both exciting and frustrating to sit at the defendant's table while being unable to call witnesses, introduce evidence, or address the jury.

I threw myself into the job. Eager to learn every aspect of being a public defender, I often accompanied the investigators when they searched witnesses or reviewed crime scenes. The work took us into some of the city's toughest, most crime-ridden neighborhoods. I really honed my observation skills and my ability to remain cool in dangerous situations.

"Laura" was my favorite member of the investigation team. A veteran of the public defender's office, she was a white woman with a slight figure, an attractively intense face, and eyes that could see right through you, sending the clear message, "Don't mess with me."

Laura taught me how to gain the confidence of potential witnesses. "You know, they don't know who we are," she explained. "We could be the police as far as they're concerned, and I'll tell ya, there is not much love for the police in the places we have to go. So my advice is to always kill 'em with kindness. Once they realize that we might be able to help someone they know, their guard drops a little and we can get the information we need without any hassles."

Laura also taught me how to blend in on an investigative run: no tie, no suit, no shiny shoes. Since investigators were forbidden to carry firearms, she taught me how to sense possible danger and take steps to protect my personal safety without showing fear or suspicion.

All of this was an interesting and valuable experience for my later career. But what I hated about the public defender job was dealing with people who didn't seem to want any help. A typical client intake interview I recall involved meeting with a kid accused of senselessly beating a woman on the street. "I have to ask why you did that," I said.

"Oh, we was just wildin', that's all," he said in a disturbingly cold voice.

"Wilding?"

"Yeah, we was just walkin' down the street and this woman was passin' by. My partnah just started beatin' on her and I joined him—like that, we was just wildin'."

Disgusted, I continued the interview and processed the young man for representation while resisting the desire to grab him and try to shake some sense into him.

The same kind of experience was repeated over and over. There was the husband who caught his wife cheating and threw acid in her face to teach her a lesson, the kid working in the department store jailed for stealing from his employer, the man who shot his next-door neighbor with his World War II rifle, and, of course, an endless stream of drug cases. These people needed and deserved representation before the criminal justice system, and that's all I was there to provide. But I admit that sometimes I felt out of place.

One morning, my intake was a tough-looking black man of intimidating build who was bound with shackles. As he took his seat across from me, the sheriffs handcuffed him to the chair. Clearly this guy was viewed as potentially dangerous. The look in his face as he glared at me made it clear that he wasn't having a good day—or a good life, for that matter.

After reviewing some information about the charges, I asked him the same question I always asked: "And you would like a public defender to represent you?"

"Nah, I don't want one of them," he said.

"You don't want an attorney?" I asked.

"Yeah, but I don't want a public defender. Y'all not real attorneys. I want a *real* attorney."

I'd had enough. "Okay, well, I'll see ya later. Sheriff, you can escort this gentleman out."

Suddenly alarmed, he interjected, "Wait a minute! I need an attorney! What are you doing?"

"Public defenders *are* real attorneys. If you don't want a public defender, then have a good day," I said. I could see the sheriff stifling his laughter.

Finally, the suspect relented. "All right, all right, I'll deal with you people if I have to. But I want him." He motioned to the white defender sitting at the intake desk next to me.

Now it was obvious what was really going on. This man wasn't uneasy about having a public defender—he was uneasy about being represented by a black attorney. I was profoundly offended. How could he show such prejudice in the situation he was in?

With each passing day, that job with the CIA sounded better and better.

Finally, the call came. The woman on the phone was very pleasant as she congratulated me on being accepted for employment with the Central Intelligence Agency. I was speechless, but somehow I managed to fumble out that I wholeheartedly accepted the offer.

I could hardly believe what was happening. All that I had gone through—the struggles at home, the search for my racial identity, the quest for a place where I belonged—all of that was behind me now. I was going to do something that would transcend any category of color or class. I was going to work for the CIA as an American, nothing more, nothing less. And I was damned proud of that.

Thankfully, Sandy was completely supportive of my decision to join the Agency—in fact, knowing how unhappy I was working with the public defender's office, she seemed as excited as I was. That night, we went out for a nice romantic dinner to celebrate. It felt wonderful to reach a pinnacle in life and have someone I loved to share it with. Even better, my family wasn't around to tarnish the moment.

Within a few days, Sandy and I packed our things and moved east to Washington, DC, where I hoped and believed a new America was waiting for me.

PART TWO

## THE AGENCY

# CHAPTER FIVE

# Joining the CIA

I JOINED THE AGENCY AS A CAREER TRAINEE IN THE DIRECTOR-ate of Operations (DO) to become a case officer—one of the foot soldiers of the clandestine service. A real-world James Bond, a case officer works around the world gathering the crucial information needed by intelligence analysts and policymakers. One job of the case officer is to find and recruit individuals who can and will provide confidential information of importance to the national security of the United States: political secrets, economic data, military information, and more. In CIA-speak, these individuals are called agents, while to the rest of the world they are known as spies.

As for me, I was determined to become one of the best case officers ever, white or black.

Like most case officers, I entered the Agency undercover. The fact that I worked for the CIA was confidential. If people asked about my job, I would explain that I worked as a US government representative. It was up to each officer individually to decide whom to tell the truth about working for the CIA, as long as it would not cause any difficulties.

I had absolutely no hesitation about hiding where I worked—in fact, I found it exciting. After all, I was accustomed to being a big mystery to just about everyone who knew me. Living undercover would be no problem for me at all.

Sandy and I arrived in the Washington, DC, area in early April 1993. Due to money constraints, we were unable to live as close to CIA headquarters as I would have liked, so we settled in an area near Dulles airport about fifteen miles west of the Capitol. The Reston/Herndon area was very inviting to a young couple making their first steps into the world. During the days before I started work, Sandy and I explored our new environs, which were amazingly different from what we were used to in St. Louis. In particular, there were many more interracial couples than we had ever seen. Sandy soon found a job with a nearby car dealership, while I prepared for one of the biggest days of my life.

It was a beautiful day in mid-May. The only memorable moment of my fifteen-mile trip to Langley, Virginia, came just at the entrance to the CIA compound. As I awaited the green light to make the turn, in the median just to my left I saw a simple little monument of two crosses and flowers. It was dedicated to two CIA employees who'd been gunned down at this very spot by a Pakistani national named Mir Aimal Kasi on January 25, 1993. I sat there, mesmerized by the memorial, until honking cars behind me reminded me to turn.

I'd already known I was going to be part of something important, and seeing that monument increased my sense of resolve and commitment.

My first stop was the visitor's center, where I joined a group of twenty or so new recruits to the Agency. I was somewhat comforted to see a melting pot of faces: black, white, Asian, and Hispanic, both men and women. Still, the atmosphere in the visitor's center was tense and the air of suspicion was overwhelming. "Need to know" was a mantra I had heard time and time again during the interview process, and I took it to heart. I didn't know any of these people, and none of them had any need to know anything about me. I wasn't going to do anything that might jeopardize what I had accomplished, and that evidently was the attitude of everyone else in the visitor's center as well. So we all sat, paced, and stared out the windows saying not a word, averting our gaze from one another, conscious of the watchful eyes of the security officers nearby.

Finally, someone from the main building came to greet us. Based on the descriptions in the recommended reading materials, as well as my lifetime of exposure to the mystique of espionage as reflected in popular culture, I had been expecting to see larger-than-life people associated with the CIA. But the woman who came to escort us to the main building was short of stature and somewhat overweight—there was nothing at all extraordinary about her appearance. She invited us to join her in a bus headed to the main building. The silence continued as we filed onto the bus and took our seats. Gazing out of the window, the first thing I noticed was how green the compound was. The buildings and the massive parking lots appeared to be isolated in a little forest, complete with jogging trails and squirrels scurrying about. I felt as if the rest of the world had been left behind at the front gate. I'd soon learn that was true in more ways than I could possibly imagine.

The bus pulled up to the front of the building, and we all eagerly got out. The neon lights in the main lobby seemed to cast a gray pallor over the scene. To my left, I saw the display of stars that formed a memorial to fallen CIA officers. Then I noticed the CIA crest on the floor in the middle of the lobby. I'd fallen a little behind the rest of the group, eagerly drinking in the entire scene. For a brief moment, as I stood there on the regal crest, everyone and everything around me disappeared. The world spun. I suddenly knew I had arrived. It was all I could do to stifle the mighty "yeah!" welling up inside me.

Following the lady from the bus, we made our way to the first of what would be many orientation classes. With our suits and our excited looks, it was obvious to everyone we passed that we were the new blood. The hallways in headquarters were wide, long, and teeming with activity. Though white males were clearly the majority, there were people of all types: women, minorities, and even some employees with disabilities. I had no idea what their positions were, but I was glad to see diversity as promised.

Otherwise, nothing seemed impressive about these people who worked at the world's premier spy agency. The women looked as if they had given up on keeping up with the latest fashions. Many of the men wore button-down, short-sleeve shirts with ties—nerdy fashion emergencies like those I'd last seen during high school.

As a newcomer to the Agency, I wanted to know everything about everyone that I saw there. But over the next few weeks, the only people I got to know were those stuck with me in the boring "welcome to the CIA" classes and the administrative sessions related to health insurance, 401(k) plans, computer training, and other mundane matters.

Over the next several months, I endured training class after training class. The goal of eventually becoming a case officer sustained me through those endless sessions. As I gradually discovered, I was one of just a handful of case officer career trainees in the group. The others were slated for technical, administrative, or analytical career tracks.

Despite my boredom and impatience, as time passed I found myself becoming more and more impressed with the Agency. There was so much to learn about: my own Directorate of Operations, as well as the Directorate of Intelligence (DI), the Directorate of Science and Technology (DS&T), and the Directorate of Administration (DA). I was fascinated by the history of the organization, intrigued by the ways in which it accomplished the job of collecting intelligence about the rest of the world, and proud of being a part of what had always been a mysterious place to me and most other Americans.

Once the orientation was completed, I finally found myself actually working in the Agency. The DO is divided into regional areas: the Near East and South Asia division (usually referred to as NE), East Asia division (EA), Africa division (AF), Central Eurasia division (CE, formerly the Soviet Eurasia division), European division (EUR), Latin America division (LA), and national resources division (NR) covering domestic field offices. There are also subject-matter divisions within the DO, such as the counterterrorism division (CT) and counter-proliferation division (CP). In-house training within the area divisions gives new recruits a direct introduction and experience in the inner workings of the Agency and its field operations.

The value of area division experience was stressed to new recruits. In particular, assignment to an overseas regional area was considered to be especially valuable to a new case officer when the time came for field assignments. However, the in-house training I received was suspiciously close to rudimentary office work. I was introduced to life in an office cubicle, the game of phone tag, and, above all, the intricacies of government bureaucracy. There were so many forms to figure out and protocols to be followed for any sort of approval that I began to wonder how anything got accomplished.

Learning the language of the Agency was an adventure in itself. Everyone spoke in acronyms, and half the time I had no idea what anyone was talking about. I wasn't a career trainee, I was a CT; my car wasn't my car, it was a POV (personally operated vehicle); the security guards were SPOs (security protective officers), and so on. Little by little, I found myself becoming accustomed to speaking in tongues—specifically, in Agency-speak.

I also couldn't help but notice the political leanings of Agency employees. I found that many if not most of my colleagues were very conservative: definitely pro-life, anti–gun control, anti–affirmative action, and anti–everything foreign or liberal. Though Bill Clinton was president, I encountered more than a few desks adorned with tributes to Ronald Reagan. Listening to one of the many Reagan disciples, one might almost think that a new religion had been founded, with the former president as God. Personally, I'd never found much appeal in Ronald Reagan. I thought that First Lady Rosalynn Carter had summed him up well in a 1979 interview with Barbara Walters: "He makes us comfortable with our prejudices." What I saw in the Agency provided a sad sort of confirmation. To many Agency employees, Reagan represented legitimization of their fears and ignorance—a mix I had difficulty seeing as conducive to the intelligence service of the United States. They continually lamented the passing of the good old days when Reagan was in charge, when the Agency could do what it wanted, where it wanted, without interference from outsiders.

Another discovery I made during those early days was the extreme compartmentalization in the world of intelligence. Analysts grouped with analysts, techs stayed in the tech crowd, and support staff knew their place. At the top of the food chain were the case officers, who socialized with no one except other case officers.

It was easy to get swept up in the mind-set of the case officer. Case officers are hired for a very particular job: to convince foreign nationals to betray their countries by giving secrets to agents of the United States. Persuading people to commit treason is a peculiar task that calls for a particular personality type. Generalizations are always dangerous, but they often have at least a grain of truth. In my experience, CIA case officers tend to be slick, manipulative, untrustworthy, and arrogant. They know their work is the very lifeblood of the Agency, and they believe that everyone else is just there to support them.

It occurred to me during my training that such arrogance might be counterproductive to an efficient intelligence agency, but I could understand it. The truth is that I was damned proud to be learning how to be part of such an exclusive club.

The separation of case officers from the rest of the Agency reflected the insular and clubby atmosphere of the entire operation. The whole chain of command resembled a military regime, with superior and inferior officers, but it was dominated by informal yet powerful cliques. To get anything done or to move up in the ranks, you had to be part of the right clique.

Once I recognized the reality of the Agency, I wasn't intimidated by it. I knew I could get in and be accepted. There was no doubt in my mind that I had what it took to become a case officer.

I had the opportunity to meet several longtime members of the case officer corps, but no acquaintance was more valuable than "Ray." I met Ray during one of my stints on the area desks. He was a white case officer who had served for forty years. I thoroughly enjoyed my lunch sessions with Ray, where he would tell me about his exploits:

working clandestinely, recruiting agents, and gathering intelligence. I gladly played the role of apprentice.

My ego certainly received a boost during one particular conversation with Ray. We were in the center courtyard of the Agency, a little oasis of grass and trees just outside the cafeteria. We were sitting at a table, and Ray had just finished describing one of his operations to me.

"You know, Ray," I said. "Based on what you've told me, it seems that being a case officer is quite an involved job. Sometimes I wonder if I will be able to do it. I really don't know what I'm getting into."

With a bit of a chuckle, Ray responded, "Jeff, let me tell you something. I've been a part of the intelligence game for a lot of years, and I've seen all kinds of case officers. From what I've seen of you and the type of work you can do, you are going to be a damned fine case officer." If I had had any doubts about my ability to succeed, they were dashed that day.

As time passed, I gradually learned that my real training was to begin once I went to the special CIA training facility universally known as the Farm. Without training at the Farm, one could not become a case officer; in fact, nothing I experienced at headquarters mattered unless and until I passed the Farm. The Farm would be the proving ground where my ability to be a case officer would be put to the test.

Along with praise of the Farm came whispers. On more than one occasion, I was told that the Farm was a place where alcoholic or otherwise troubled case officers were sent as a sort of personal exile for them to get their act together. I brushed those rumors aside. I decided that my experience at the Farm was going to be a positive one, with quality instructors who would immediately recognize my potential as a case officer. I became more and more impatient to complete my in-house training and move on to the Farm.

About a month after my entrance on duty (EOD, in Agency-speak) I finally got to meet other case-officers-to-be who were going to be in my class at the Farm. I once again took comfort in the fact that they were not all white males. There were three new recruits in particular whom I more or less clicked with: "Rachel," "Curtis," and "Fernando."

Rachel was of American Indian descent, Curtis was black, and Fernando was Hispanic. Despite the fact that we had each taken very different paths to the CIA, we forged an almost immediate bond.

One day Curtis, Fernando, and I met in the cafeteria for lunch. As we were making our way to a table, we were summoned by a dapper-looking black gentleman sitting at a table near a window. He invited us to lunch with him, and we accepted. "Henderson" was a veteran of the Agency with thirty-plus years of experience. He had a cosmopolitan air about him, with a very proper speaking voice, gentlemanly mannerisms, and coordinated business attire. Henderson told us about his background, which included a PhD from Yale, and asked us what we thought so far about the Agency. Then he dropped a bombshell of a question on me.

"Jeffrey," he said "you have a law degree. What are you doing here? You could take that degree, go anywhere you want, and do much better than you will here."

I didn't quite know how to respond. Henderson elaborated with a serious look on his face. "I've been here for over thirty years, and I'll tell you something: nothing has changed when it comes to race. You might see a lot of black folks around here, but I guarantee you most of them are janitors or support staff. The fact that the three of you are in the case officer training program is remarkable in and of itself. They don't normally let many of us into that career track."

Now that the subject of race had been broached, Henderson spent the rest of the lunch telling us about how the Agency was filled with nothing but southern-style good old boys and how it was a difficult place for black employees, regardless of their career or status. He concluded, "This is the only place I can think of where a white man with a high school education will go farther than a black man with a PhD."

Henderson left the three of us with something troubling to think about. But, like the others, I found what he had said hard to believe. It didn't make any sense to me. I wondered, if working at the Agency has been so difficult for Henderson, why had he been here for so long?

I thought about that conversation a lot after that. Henderson's comments made me more sensitive to some things I might have been inclined to overlook. I noticed that most of the managers I met were white males. Discreet questioning revealed that the black faces I saw in the building mostly belonged to secretaries or janitors, just as Henderson had said. I'd heard that there were other black case officers like me, but I never actually met one. The black employees who weren't case officers seemed to have no idea what to make of me. When I did meet other black people, I always felt their unease.

One black woman I met, a finance specialist, told me that, at first, she and her friends had decided I must be arrogant. "We thought you just wanted to be with them white folks," she said. "We thought you were all uppity because you were a case officer." But then she softened: "Now I can tell that you're not like that at all, you're just sort of the quiet type."

I didn't know how to react, so I said nothing. I told myself I was there to do my job, not to win a popularity contest. But I was disturbed.

Afterward, I made it a point to ask about black case officers, and the answer I got was usually the same: "We do have black case officers, but they are mainly in the field."

I also asked the same question of Henderson some weeks later. His answer was not as satisfying. "Black case officers?" He chuckled as he continued, "There are a few around, but trust me, there aren't that many."

"Every time I ask about them," I said, "I'm told that they are in the field."

"Well, there are a few. Maybe around ten to fifteen. And that's counting the three or four members of your class who are black."

This was not at all like the vision I'd absorbed from my readings and from the interview process. But I wasn't fazed. Maybe the CIA wasn't as diverse as I'd been led to believe. But maybe I and the other black trainees would show the whole Agency that black officers can be a valuable resource for the intelligence field. I liked the idea of being a trailblazer.

✻

ALL THE WHILE, it was comforting having Sandy in my life. I'd heard stories of officers whose wives didn't know that they were married to an officer with the CIA. To me, that was completely ridiculous and not a good basis for a lasting relationship or marriage. I wasn't yet married to Sandy, but I couldn't imagine keeping my job a secret from her. As part of my hiring process, she'd been subject to a full investigation, which confirmed my assumption that she was not a foreign spy. It was nice to be able to be open with her about routine aspects of my job, though I didn't tell her about anything that was classified. Even keeping that limited array of secrets from her did not sit well with me.

Sandy was pretty happy with her administrative job at a nearby car dealership. She also got involved as a volunteer coach with some girls' fast-pitch softball teams, a sport she had excelled at in high school and college. Working with the kids made her extremely happy, and she recruited me to help as her assistant coach. It was fun spending time with Sandy doing something that she loved, even when, during batting practice, I got hit by a pitch under my left eye. Trying to maintain my composure with a steady stream of blood pouring down my face, I turned it into a teaching moment: "Now see, kids—this is why you wear a helmet."

All in all, the summer of 1993 was a time of tremendous personal excitement for me. I was on my way to becoming a success in a new career, and I had someone very special to share it with. Sandy and I were falling more and more in love with each other during that summer. We ate out, went to amusement parks, explored the big city, made friends in our neighborhood, and enjoyed it all together. We were the kind of stable, caring, sharing couple I had never seen growing up. I was determined to not be like my parents and the others I grew up with in Cape, and I was doing it.

As the year progressed, I finally felt it was time to make Sandy my wife. Lacking the funds for a cozy, charming wedding with all the trimmings like the ones I had seen on television, we arranged to tie the knot in a simple civil ceremony on December 1, 1993. We hoped to have a formal wedding in either her hometown or mine once my training was over.

My mother's response was anything but elated. When I shared our plans with her by phone, "that's nice" was all she had to say. I could sense she wanted to say something more, and I half expected her to criticize me for wanting to marry a white girl. I can only imagine the disappointment the rest of the family must have felt when she told them the news. In their eyes, I had left them behind for the white man's world.

I wished it was different. But, in truth, the feelings of my mother and the rest of my family were of little concern to me. I was proud of the fact that I was making it on my own terms, not those dictated by the color of my skin.

>‹

By mid-1994, I was pleased when I was scheduled to finally go to the Farm. I'd absorbed all I could from over a year of endless in-house training, and the routine was beginning to wear on me. The numbers and makeup of my class had finally been determined. Much to my surprise, though our class was small—just about a third of the traditional size, I was told—it was actually pretty diverse. Along with me, Curtis, Fernando, and Rachel, we gained more women, a couple more Hispanic people, and a few more black men. Of course, the white men in our group remained the majority, but there were enough others to add some flavor to the class. Those of us in the minority jokingly dubbed ourselves "the quota class," and we bonded immediately.

During the drive down to the Farm, I was relieved to be finally starting real training to be a case officer. I was also quite nervous. Newly married, it was tough knowing I would be away from Sandy for months. Most importantly, I knew that those months were going to make or break my future with the Agency.

Much like headquarters, the Farm was self-contained and shielded from the outside world. Even more than when I'd arrived at headquarters for the first time, I felt as if I was entering another world when I entered the Farm.

Once my classmates and I settled into the facility, we met the instructors and quickly developed a sense of us against them. Not only did they represent the gatekeepers we needed to get past in order to join an exclusive club, but we couldn't ignore the fact that we looked nothing like them. Other than one part-time, semiretired black instructor, all the instructors at the Farm were white. They were also thoroughly unimpressive. The strongest impression I had was not about their expertise, experience, or wisdom, but about their determination to whip us into shape, the way fraternity officers do to young pledges.

Each trainee was assigned an instructor who was to offer one-on-one coaching during training. Mine was "Dave," a man of short stature and a strong resemblance to former vice president Dan Quayle.

Dave introduced himself genially, saying, "We've found that it can be beneficial for students to have a mentor, especially during this tough course. I want you to know that, should you have any problems, you can come to me any time."

I responded, "I appreciate your offer, but, to be honest with you, I doubt I'll be coming to you much if at all. I'm here to be a case officer, and I have to be able to do it on my own."

I was very clear about the reason for my statement. I wanted to leave no doubt in anyone's mind that I had what it took to become a case officer—and that I wasn't intimidated by the fact that I would be held at a higher standard simply because I was black. Dave reacted with a bit of a confused look. I suppose I came across as arrogant. But maybe in some way I gained his respect that day.

Training started—day after day of learning the tools and trade of the case officer. There was so much to learn: surveillance; how to find, recruit, and exploit agents; the proper format for communications with headquarters; and, most importantly, the varieties and proper use of cover—the false persona that opens doors of operational opportunity for the case officer in the field. Without the proper cover as a government official or businessman and the relevant credentials to make the cover appear genuine, a case officer cannot perform in the field. I found the idea of cover both very interesting and natural. I had always been good at putting on whatever face was necessary for me to survive in a given situation.

Though we case officer candidates were immersed in the world of the Farm, there were a couple of events in the outside world that we couldn't help taking notice of. One was a class-action suit against the Agency that had been filed by a group of female case officers charging discrimination on account of gender. The case had been brewing for some time, but talk of a settlement reignited conversation on the topic while I was at the Farm. In the mess hall at lunchtime, it was routine to hear the instructors disparaging the women who'd filed the suit as troublemakers motivated solely by greed.

Still, it was obvious that the Agency took the issue of gender fairness seriously. Our program included a session of sensitivity training on sexual harassment. In addition, a special class was convened for the students to hear from a longtime female employee, who spoke on the role of women in the CIA. After recounting a few highlights of her career, she defended the Agency against charges that women had limited opportunities by saying, "There are places in the world where a woman just cannot operate effectively as a case officer due to cultural limitations." I'm sure there's truth in this argument. But what the speaker had to say might have made more of an impact if she'd ever served in more than a supporting position; the fact is, she'd never been a case officer herself.

The other event making headlines while I was at the Farm was the case of Aldrich "Rick" Ames, a CIA officer who'd sold US secrets to the Soviet Union. But unlike the women's lawsuit, the Ames case was almost never mentioned at the Farm. As an aspiring case officer and an outsider working hard to earn a place on the inside, I was curious about the situation. I wanted to know how something like this could happen. What would make a CIA officer betray the organization and his country in this way? I thought it would have been a good subject for us to discuss—if only as a cautionary tale—but the clear message sent by the silence of our instructors was that a member of the club had fallen from grace, and that it would have been something close to sacrilege even to comment on his dishonor.

After months of training, exercises, report writing, sleepless nights, and fattening mess-hall food, the training program concluded with a written exam. On a crisp December day, the candidates were summoned to their mentors' offices one by one to be told whether they'd passed or failed.

The moment I entered Dave's office, he congratulated me. A feeling of relief flooded through me.

"You know, at the beginning of the course, many of us instructors wondered whether you were going to be able to make it," Dave said. "But in the end, you did quite well."

I wanted to yell, "I told you so!" Instead, I just smiled and thanked him.

That evening, a ceremony and dinner was held for those who'd passed the exam—about two-thirds of the class. A crusty old veteran case officer came down from headquarters to regale us with stories of his career triumphs. The next day, we were released from the shackles of the Farm, and I returned home to Sandy, feeling like a conquering hero. Given the fact that my new career could be shared with no one in my family, nor with anyone else outside the Agency, I felt blessed to have at least one person in the world to share my achievement with.

Such was the path I'd chosen to walk. Now, I'd been officially accepted—and I loved it.

# CHAPTER SIX

# Shadow of Africa

WHEN I RETURNED TO LANGLEY AFTER COMPLETING MY training at the Farm, the atmosphere was not the same. Now that I was a certified case officer—not just a legitimate staff member, but one of the Agency's elite—I expected to feel more a part of the place, more a member of the team. But when I checked into Near East and South Asia division, I felt anything but welcome. I was greeted with suspicion, as if my colleagues were welcoming not simply a new case officer but the new *black* case officer—a very different matter.

I was assigned to the Iran desk within the NE division at headquarters. Although I considered this the most desirable posting in the Agency, I was disappointed that my new job was in Langley rather than overseas. I had never traveled to a foreign country, and I was longing to go abroad.

For an American spy, few targets are more interesting than Iran. Ever since the revolution in 1979, Iranian society has been cut off from the West. For years, even American tourists weren't allowed into the country. The United States desperately needs any window it can get into the Iranian regime. One reason is that Iran is a major sponsor of terrorist groups, such as Hezbollah, the organization that carried out the 1982 suicide attack on the Marine Corps barracks in Lebanon, killing 241 American servicemen. We also know that the Iranian government is doing its utmost to acquire nuclear weapons. Given Iran's implacable hostility toward the United States—it was the Iranian mullahs, after all, who coined the phrase "the Great Satan" to describe the United States—the prospect of a nuclear-armed Iran should frighten any thinking American.

What's more, Iran represents a daunting challenge to American spycraft. The Iranian intelligence service has gained skills and confidence since the revolution, and has indeed become one of the world's best-trained, most ruthless, and most professional espionage organizations. Virtually all Iranian citizens with access to the regime's secrets have been thoroughly indoctrinated to hate and fear the United States and particularly the CIA, and many are terrified of speaking to Americans when they travel overseas, if they're even allowed such travel. For all these reasons, gathering intelligence about Iran is probably one of the hardest jobs in the business. That was fine with me—I wanted the hardest job.

When I went to my new office to introduce myself, I realized that, once again, mine would be the only black face in the group—a familiar role, though one I never expect to feel comfortable with. I was fortunate enough to be thrust into the action from my very first day on the Iran desk. When I arrived, the chief of the section and his deputy were leaving for other assignments, and the office was in disarray. This created a window of opportunity for me. Despite the fact that I had just graduated from the Farm, I became involved in some sensitive cases. Within a few months, at the age of twenty-seven, I was an important part of the Iran desk. I was exhilarated. It felt like a natural culmination of my childhood and the many hours I spent glued to the television during the Iran hostage crisis.

Still, I was frustrated about the fact that I was stuck at a desk in Langley rather than working overseas. So I was delighted when, a few months after I joined the NE division, I was told I would be sent abroad. I was to take a short trip to Africa and ███████████████

███████████████████████████████████████████████
███████████████████████████████████████████████
███████████████████████████████████████████████
███████████████████████████████████████████████
███████████████████████████████████████████████
███████████████████████████████████████████████
███████████████████████████████████████████████.

In the days before my trip, I was almost too excited to sit still—not just because I would be going overseas for the first time in my life, but because of where I would be going. Like most black Americans, I had grown up believing that I was somehow personally connected to Africa. When I was in college, Afrocentrism was at the height of its popularity. Many of the people I know wore African medallions or gave their children African names—symbols of a sense of ethnic pride that I shared with them.

My destination of Liberia was also significant for me. Settled in 1822 by freed American slaves, Liberia symbolizes the dream of returning to one's African roots. As I planned my trip, I was hoping, perhaps half unconsciously, that in Africa I would finally find a place where I felt at home, naturally at ease, accepted as simply another person in the crowd.

When my departure date finally arrived, I was overwhelmed with excitement. As I boarded the Air Afrique jet after a layover in Paris, I found myself filled with wonder. *Good God*, I thought, *we really do have our own airline!* I loved the fact that the pilot and the entire flight crew were black. Usually, I find flying boring and fall asleep as soon as the plane takes off. This time, I was wide awake the entire flight, my body humming with excitement. Other case officers had regaled me with horror stories about African airlines: "The bathrooms are disgusting." "Be prepared to sit next to a flock of goats." "Don't be surprised if your plane loses a wing while you're in the air." But I was unconcerned, and in fact the flight was uneventful, which quietly validated my sense of racial pride. I studied the monitor showing the plane's flight path with rapt attention, and when the little animated plane sailed into African airspace, waves of emotion shimmered up and down my spine.

We stopped for a brief scheduled layover in Bamako, Mali. When the plane landed, I remained in my seat for a few minutes, but finally I could take it no longer. I asked the flight attendant if I could get off the plane and look around. "I *have* to, because this is my first trip to Africa!"

The flight attendant had a pretty smile, and when she said, "Welcome to Africa" in an enchanting accent, I felt as if the whole continent was stretching out its arms to embrace me. She ushered me toward the cabin door so I could step for the first time on the soil of Africa—the motherland.

We flew on to Abidjan in the Ivory Coast, where I would be meeting another case officer who would show me the ropes. When I departed the plane, the first thing I noticed was the heat and the humidity—far more intense than I'd been accustomed to as a boy growing up on the banks of the Mississippi. The airport consisted of a small dilapidated building, a burned-out jeep, and an apology for a flight tower. A handful of people seemed to be hanging about aimlessly by the building and chatting. In the distance, the landscape was wide and arid, dotted with sparse greenery. There was no jungle, there were no elephants, and Marlin Perkins was nowhere to be seen.

To my astonishment, the area around the airport reminded me of the street corner on any given night in my hometown. The faces of the Africans were the same as the faces I knew back home. Their body language was the same. They looked just like the guys on the street in my neighborhood, the ones who told animated stories about the women they'd conquered the night before and their daily brushes with the Man. Only the oppressive heat and the barren landscape told me I was not in Cape Girardeau.

After looking at the people around me in puzzlement for a few moments, I reached a simple conclusion: "I guess that people are basically the same all over the world."

Abidjan was also not what I'd expected. This was no cozy village with mud huts and scratching chickens, and there wasn't a loincloth to be had for love or money. It was a bustling city, with traffic jams, packed restaurants, and streets filled with people arguing and shouting. I was transfixed. This was what I'd hoped to see—not savannahs and safaris, but the real life of ordinary African men and women. It was emotionally stunning for me to be surrounded by black people, not members of a minority or an underclass, but simply the thousands of characters in the cast of a big city—upper-class people, lower-class people, police officers, sanitation workers, businessmen, women with shopping bags, children in school uniforms, passersby. All were black, and none were different for being so.

Before turning in for the night, I walked the city streets for hours. Little by little, I noticed something odd. When you're black in the United States, you usually have an instant rapport with other black people, no matter where you go. It's like being part of a special club. When two black people pass each other in the street, they nod, smile, or say hello, always sending the same unspoken message: "Hey, you're black! So am I! Glad I'm not alone."

But as I walked down the street in Abidjan, I was surprised to feel the same cold indifference from passersby as I do when I pass white people on the streets in America. I had expected to feel a sense of belonging, but somehow I knew instantly that I didn't belong there at all. It seemed as if everyone who saw me knew that too.

In Abidjan, I connected with "Frank," who had been in Africa for most of his career. He was the first black case officer I'd ever met. I was eager to hear about his experiences, and we talked until late in the night. His view of the Agency was deeply discouraging. He told me that most of the crucial CIA stations in Africa were staffed almost entirely by white officers—men who attracted crowds of curious onlookers just by stepping out their front doors. In fact, there wasn't a single black officer in that particular African country, he told me. Frank struggled against the unavoidable impression that the CIA kept a handful of black officers on its books only to fill quotas and deflect lawsuits. "They've got to show that there are at least a few of us out here," he said. "And a few is all it will ever be."

I hoped he was wrong. Times were changing, I thought privately, and I had the chance to be a pioneer. If I led the way, other black men and women would follow. I didn't say this to Frank, of course. It would have sounded arrogant.

The next morning, we were scheduled to fly to Monrovia, the capital of Liberia, on Wesua Airlines. Wesua's fleet seemed to be comprised of antiquated Russian propeller planes piloted by equally antiquated Soviet military veterans. The flight was delayed by almost two hours, but I didn't mind; I sat in the airport, where the air felt close and sticky because there was no air conditioning, and took in the scene full of black travelers. Back home in Cape, people laughed at the idea of flying. "I ain't getting' in no plane," I'd heard friends and family say when I was growing up. "I'll keep my feet on the ground. It's white folks like to fly." These Africans were flying, like white folks, just as I always knew they could, and it was good to see.

Finally, the plane was ready. The entry door was so tiny that I nearly had to crawl through it. The inside of the plane reminded me of a Greyhound bus, tight and cramped with a low ceiling. There were no seat assignments, so I took a seat next to a window. Frank sat in front of me and the flight attendant behind me. A few of the seats across the aisle had been yanked up and stacked in the corner; in their place was a blue tarp.

Once everyone was aboard, the flight attendant stepped over the luggage in the aisle and walked to the front of the plane. "Thank you for flying Wesua Airlines today to Monrovia," he began. "Please do not be alarmed if you see what looks like steam once we are in the air and turn on the air conditioner. It is merely condensation rising in the cabin. Enjoy the flight."

I gazed wide-eyed out of the window as the plane taxied and climbed. Frank pointed outside. "Notice that we're flying along the coast?" he asked. "That's so no one will shoot a surface-to-air missile at us."

"Really?" I replied weakly, wondering why no one had mentioned this possibility to me before.

Despite Frank's unsettling comment, I was overwhelmed by the beauty of the scenery outside the plane: waves crashing on the shore under a vibrant dark-blue sky. Suddenly I realized to my horror that great plumes of white smoke were billowing up in the cabin. I clutched the armrests, wondering whether I was the only one who saw that smoke and why the hell everyone else was so damned calm. I was about to tap Frank's shoulder to demand an explanation when I realized that this was what the flight attendant must have meant by "steam." No one else around me seemed to find it at all remarkable.

A throng of people was waiting for us on the ground, including a State Department official from the local embassy who had come to greet us. "I was wondering when you were going to get here," he said. "I'd heard that you were going to be late because of the diplomat."

"What diplomat?" I asked.

"The Liberian diplomat who just died in the United States. His body was on your flight."

All of a sudden I understood the meaning of that blue tarp, and I felt slightly nauseated.

My initial image of Monrovia was appealing. I was charmed by the sight of low, whitewashed buildings against the vibrant palm trees and greenery, all bathed in a glowing, almost Mediterranean light. But when I arrived in the heart of the city, these hints of beauty vanished. Years of civil war had left Monrovia a burned-out ruin, lacking regular electricity and running water. Only the restaurants and hotels with private generators, mostly owned by Lebanese expatriates, had power. Most buildings were riddled with bullet holes, their windows blasted out of their panes. Squatters languished and rats scuttered amid the burned and bomb-ravaged shell of the royal palace. My first impression was merely a sad glimpse of what the place might have been.

The people of Monrovia were charming, despite the ravages that had befallen their city. They smiled often and seemed warm and accepting. I was fascinated by the physical differences, and similarities, between Africans and black Americans. It wasn't just that their skin was darker; it seemed to me that they were of a more luminous and striking hue, somehow more intense. Their average height was about the same as that of black Americans, but they were far thinner. But, apart from their sandals, they dressed the same way black people do in the United States. I didn't see what I'd always imagined to be traditional African dress, the kind that professors of African studies liked to wear to class—vibrant prints, elaborate headdresses. Instead I saw Levis and Air Jordans. Again, I concluded with a touch of dismay that people were the same all over the world.

But if the Liberians resembled Americans on the surface, that impression changed once I spoke to them. After a few days there, I found some free hours to do a bit of exploring. I wanted to go alone, but the embassy officials insisted that I take a local escort. His name was "Togar," and he was a Monrovian police officer—a thankless career in a city where the very idea of law and order was a joke. Togar took me around the city to see the sights, explaining the history of local landmarks in a macabre simulacrum of a tour guide's patter: "Here, this section of the city about two years ago, big massacre. The Krahn control this neighborhood. They are very dangerous. And *this* neighborhood is where Charles Taylor's men caught Samuel Doe. They tortured him pretty good for everyone to see. They even cut his ears off before they take him down to the beach to shoot him."

Togar took me to see how beautiful the beach was. Turquoise waves lapped against the fine, iridescent sand; swaying palms were animated by the gentle breeze. But there wasn't a soul on the beach. I asked why. "Well," he explained, "when a tribal group captures someone they don't like, they bring him here to kill him." This evidently spoiled the beach party mood.

Togar explained that warring factions often raided villages controlled by rival tribes. They would round up the villagers and interrogate them about their tribal allegiance. In one recent raid, a soldier had grabbed a pregnant woman by the arm. "Hey there, mama, what you got there in your belly?"

The terrified woman replied, "How I'm supposed to know that? It not born yet!"

"Well, I got a way I can find out," said the soldier. He turned to one of his compatriots. "Hey, mon, what you bet me this woman carrying a son?"

The other soldier accepted the bet. "I say she got a girl in there." The first soldier promptly sliced the woman open with a knife and snatched out the unborn baby.

"Ha, ha! Told you it was a boy," he announced.

Togar seemed to take an odd delight in telling me these disgusting stories. In his whole life, he had known nothing but civil war and horror. It seemed that every inch of Monrovia had been marked by cruelty and savagery.

The Economic Community of West African States (ECOWAS) had sent peacekeeping troops, who manned armed checkpoints on the road where cars were routinely stopped for inspection. I'd been warned that ignoring these checkpoints could be fatal. But as we drove around the city, Togar couldn't be bothered to stop. When we passed a checkpoint, he sailed right past the armed guards. Glancing in the rearview mirror, I saw a soldier waving his hands and raising his AK-47, but as he took aim, another soldier ran up to stop him.

I was angry and upset, but I tried to keep my voice as calm as possible. "Didn't want to stop, huh, Togar?"

"I guess he didn't see the flag," said Togar with a shrug. He meant the tiny American flag affixed to the lower corner of the windshield.

At the end of the day, we headed toward a neighborhood on the outskirts of town, named Red Light because it had the only intersection within miles with a traffic light—though the light itself hadn't worked for years. It was a lively community of homes and shops and open-air markets; despite the ever-present poverty, it seemed that Liberia had a vibrant commercial life, which is perhaps another way of saying that every Liberian was trying to sell me something. Kids on the street were hawking everything from cassava to clothing; every home had a display of eggs or homemade delicacies for purchase.

Togar led me to a "conversation hut," a kind of round open-air shelter under a roof of palm leaves, where we sat down on one of the benches. This was my first chance to chat with ordinary Monrovians. I struck up a conversation with an affable middle-aged woman named "Esther," who Togar told me was the widow of an assassinated states-man, a victim of Liberia's factional warfare. Since her husband's death, she had become a venerable Monrovian matriarch, assisting displaced families and campaigning for the formation of a stable Liberian gov-ernment. She was easy to talk to. There was something about her, in fact, that instantly reminded me of my mother.

I asked Esther when she thought the fighting in Liberia would stop. "We are waiting for *you*," she replied cheerfully. "We are waiting for the US to come and bring some order to this country."

"Well," I said truthfully, "until the civil war stops, the US won't take much of an interest in Liberia."

"The killing won't stop until a hand forceful enough to bring or-der establishes itself in this country," Esther insisted. "The US could do that very easily," she added, taking another sip from her beer.

"It's a vicious circle," I replied. "One thing won't happen until the other does, but no one is willing to make the first move."

She laughed. "Well, don't be expecting the killing to stop anytime soon. You know, we kill ourselves better than anyone." The other Afri-cans in the conversation hut chuckled in agreement.

The Red Light locals then took turns explaining Liberian tribal politics to me. Most Liberians belonged to indigenous tribes—the Krahn, the Kru, and the Gola. The Congomen, on the other hand, were descendants of the American slaves who'd originally founded the nation. Those freed slaves had applied the lessons they'd learned in America and set about enslaving the indigenous tribespeople, whom they considered mere savages.

Later that week, I discovered that Togar earned a tidy second in-come moonlighting as a pimp. We were joined one night by one of his ladies, who cooked a stew for us made using aging fish from the local market and handfuls of some kind of indigenous plant that grew around the abandoned buildings near the US embassy. The stew reeked like a rotting corpse, but Frank shoveled it down as if it were the greatest thing he'd ever tasted. I begged off a second helping, explaining that travel had upset my delicate stomach.

I was heading to my room to retire after dinner when Togar stopped me and asked what kind of woman I'd like. "Big, small, skinny? Whatever you prefer, I will get for you tonight," he offered grandly.

I thanked him and declined.

After a few weeks in Liberia, I felt I'd achieved my mission. I'd walked freely around African cities at all hours of the day and night without arousing any suspicion or questions. I'd even been offered weed by the guys hanging out on the street corners, something that I doubt happened to the white case officers.

Within a few months, I was sent back to Africa. I was excited about the prospect of taking my first crack at real espionage. My target was an Iranian man in Lagos, Nigeria, whom we knew from an informant to be desperately short of cash. Someone friendly to the CIA knew the Iranian in question and agreed to contrive a meeting between us. My job was to gauge the target's potential for recruitment as an intelligence asset. If he seemed amenable, I was authorized to pitch him.

I found Lagos to be a dirty, mean-spirited city, its air thick with leaded gas fumes and its streets just as thick with sour-looking crowds. The houses of the wealthy were protected by ugly concrete walls bearing the words "Do Not Urinate Here." The entire city reminded me of the desolate areas of St. Louis where, as a public defender, I had looked for witnesses who would testify on behalf of my clients—the parts of the city that police officers avoided and ambulance drivers wouldn't enter on a dare.

A port city built on a collection of islands, Lagos is divided by several rivers. My first glimpse of the water reminded me of skipping stones on the Mississippi as a boy, until I saw a swollen human corpse float by. Shocked, I looked around at the passersby. No one was offering the body even a glance. I stopped one man and asked him how a dead body could just float down the river without generating the slightest interest. "Well, if you touch the body, you have to take responsibility for it," he explained. "So no one touch it."

I spent my first few days in Lagos exploring the city. One day, I wandered into a local drinking hole far from my operational area. It looked like the dives I'd seen in rough neighborhoods in the States. Placards from concerts and soccer matches decorated the walls. The long countertop and stools were covered in cracked, colorful vinyl. Behind the bar were bottles of every kind of alcohol known to man. Tables and chairs were strewn about the floor haphazardly, the windows were covered, and the only light came from the colored lamps.

It was early in the evening, and the handful of patrons were fixated on the soccer match on television, a World Cup qualifying match against Liberia. I ordered a beer, took a seat at the bar, and struck up a conversation with the man next to me. "I never understood the appeal of soccer," I admitted. "I mean, it's a decent sport. But how can you get excited about a match that ends in a tie?"

Overhearing me, a tallish man to my right interjected. "You know, when you see a match that ends with no score, you know that was a good match. Very competitive." Knowing that no local would ever question the self-evident virtues of soccer, he eyed me closely. "Where you from?" he finally asked. "You look like you could be, maybe, Saudi?"

Realizing that no one in the bar was of intelligence interest, and knowing I'd never see him again, I figured I'd tell him the truth. "I'm from the US," I answered.

Hearing this, the bartender leaped into the conversation. "You're from America," he said. "All right, let me ask you something. All the time, we see on the TV that those black people in America are trying to regain their African heritage with the clothes, the music, and the trips over here." He leaned over for emphasis, looked me directly in the eye, and then asked the most sensible question I'd ever heard.

"Why," he asked, "do you want to come *here*, when all we're trying to do is get *there*?"

A man at the far end of the bar added his two cents: "Yeah. It make no sense for you to try to be African. You not African black man, you *white* black man."

The insight struck me like a thunderclap. The identity I was seeking may have its roots in Africa, but my home was America, with all the richness and beauty of the culture black Americans represented. From that moment on, I was reluctant to be referred to as African American. I found more personal meaning in being an American who is also proud to be black. I felt even more determined to find my place and be accepted in America on my terms.

The intelligence operation that had brought me to Lagos didn't end as we'd hoped. I spent almost a week trying to lure the Iranian out of his cave, but to no avail. For some reason he didn't want to come out to play, supposedly "too busy" to meet me, according to our go-between. I found this rather odd, but when I shared the story with my colleagues back at the Iran desk, they took it in stride.

I soon learned that many intelligence operations end in failure. In fact, it's probably for the best that nothing happened on my trip to Lagos. Several months later, it was discovered that the go-between was bad, probably working for the Iranians himself and trying to set me up for exposure. After learning that, I decided that I would always trust my own intuition, rather than assume that my CIA colleagues knew what they were doing.

I would make one more trip to Africa as a case officer. This time, I came tantalizingly close to making a real intelligence breakthrough.

The CIA had heard about another Iranian national who was supposed to be desperate for cash. "He's ripe for a cold pitch," I was told—an attempt, usually unsuccessful, to meet with a target and convince him to commit espionage on the spot. It's about as easy to pull off as walking up to a beautiful stranger at a party and convincing her to leave with you. Still, it was worth a try, and I flew to Iran to make the attempt. By this time, I'd learned Farsi, the national language of Iran. I was counting on this knowledge as a valuable asset that would increase my chances of success exponentially.

The people at the local station met me at my hotel and warned me about the risks that the operation entailed. "If he figures out that you're CIA and that you've tricked him into a one-on-one," someone told me, "he might get violent."

"We're not sure if he's packing," another officer said, "but just in case, take this." He offered me a stun gun.

I refused the weapon. "Don't worry about me," I said. "If he so much as looks at me funny, I'll be on him so fast he won't know what hit him. You'll have to come in and pull me off of him." I hoped it wouldn't come to that, but I was definitely prepared for the possibility. I was feeling aggressive, full of adrenaline, maybe because of the pent-up energy from the months I'd spent waiting for an opportunity to test my skills.

I called the Iranian target, introduced myself, and explained, "I'm moving to this country for business, and I need a car. I heard you have one for sale. Can we talk about it?" After a moment's hesitation, he agreed to meet me. Even as we spoke, a surveillance team from our station was watching his movements.

I waited with the other officers in my hotel room until our surveillance team called. "He's on his way to the hotel," they told me. "But bad news—he's not alone. He's got his bodyguard and his wife. Do we abort?"

"No way!" I said. "Let's see what happens." I was way too hyped up to call it off. We'd rented the room next door as well, and the other officers went there so they could cover me in an emergency.

In a few moments, there was a knock on the door, and I greeted my target. "The car is right outside," he told me. "Come downstairs and you can look it over."

We went outside, where the target's wife and bodyguard were waiting. She was nondescript, but the bodyguard was a husky brute with a mean, battle-worn face, and he didn't look as if he liked me much. I went through the motions of checking out the car, kicking the tires, sitting in the front seat, looking under the hood. The only thing it looked fit for to me was the scrap heap. The tires were balding remnants, the interior was dirty and cracked, the engine was filthy, and the body was scratched and dented. All the while, the bodyguard was staring at me and patting the conspicuous bulge under his jacket.

"How about a test drive?" the target asked me.

"Not necessary," I replied. "The car looks sensational to me." What he didn't know was that I had to decline—I can't drive a stick shift. More importantly, I needed to get him alone, away from his dutiful wife and that monster of a bodyguard. I asked him to join me for a cup of tea in the hotel restaurant so we could negotiate.

He clearly didn't feel comfortable, but he told his wife and bodyguard to stay outside with the car. That was an excellent sign, I felt.

Over our tea, we made small talk for a few minutes. Then I asked him how much he wanted for the car. He chuckled and made what we both knew was an outrageous request: "Thirty-five hundred dollars," he said, cocking his head and squinting slyly.

"Well," I replied, "that sounds like a fair price to me. I have the money in cash. It's in my room, if you want to do the deal now."

His eyes widened with surprise and greed. "You have the money in your room?"

"I told you," I said. "I'm here to buy a car, and that is precisely what I intend to do."

"Well then!" he said, his face creasing into an expression of avaricious glee. "I think we have a deal. I'll just send my wife and my friend away."

*Yes!* I thought with delight. *Let's get rid of the witnesses and have a real talk, you greedy little bastard.*

Speaking in Farsi, he ordered the bodyguard to take his wife home (not knowing, of course, that I could understand every word). Then I escorted him to my room. I'd set up a hidden camera in the wall, and I invited him to take a seat right in front of it, while I sat across the table from him. I'd positioned a briefcase nearby, making sure that some of the cash it contained was visible. Sure enough, his eyes immediately locked on the briefcase. These were all tactics I'd learned at the Farm. I was finally getting an opportunity to put them to use.

We made a bit of small talk, and I offered him a glass of water. Then the moment had come. I took a deep breath.

"Sir," I said, addressing him in Farsi, "I must confess that I am not in the least interested in your car. But I do have a business offer for you, and I assure you that it will be even more interesting, financially."

Upon hearing me speak his native language, his eyes nearly popped out of his head. His whole body went rigid, and sweat formed instantly on his brow. For a moment, he was paralyzed. With both hands clenching the glass of water, he took a couple of very deliberate sips. Then he stood up, flung open the hotel room door, and tried to flee.

But I stopped him just outside the door and immediately turned on the charm. I quickly explained what I had in mind and began to apply every persuasive technique I'd learned to convince him to accept my offer. I threw every angle at him—not just the money he would make but also his religion, his family, and the opportunity for him to help promote positive regime change in his country. I tried to play upon his purported greed as well as his conscience.

We talked in the hallway for a good while. He stood listening to me, hands in his pockets, his head down, nodding in affirmation at the various points and assurances I offered. For a moment, I had the feeling that he trusted me, and I thought he was ready to return to the room with me and strike a deal. But in the end, even if he believed me, he was unable to accept what might happen if we worked together. He politely apologized and excused himself. Still energized yet somewhat dejected, I returned to the hotel room.

Our surveillance team tracked the target as he sprinted through the streets of the city. Believing that he was likely to report what had happened to the Iranian government promptly, the station officers decided that I had to get out of the country immediately. Otherwise, I would probably be arrested—and since I was in the country for the

CIA, that would have been no joke. I hated the idea of giving up the mission, but the station officers talked sense into me and got me out of there before nightfall.

When my colleagues at headquarters heard about my exploit, they told me I'd done a great job. They were impressed with the way I'd gotten rid of the wife and bodyguard and succeeded in luring the target to my room. In fact, they later used the videotape I'd made of the episode to train other case officers in how to make a cold pitch. But I remained disappointed. I'd come so close, and yet no deal. Such is the reality of a case officer's life.

><

ON A SUBSEQUENT trip to Cape Girardeau, I had a conversation with some of the neighbors who habitually idled away their afternoons in my mother's living room. "We need to get back to being African," one man said. "Only then will black folks here remember who they are, and take back their pride in themselves."

"Have you ever been to Africa?" I asked.

"No, but I guess you have," he replied with a smirk.

"As a matter of fact," I answered, "I have been to Africa, and I can tell you that you'd be no more welcome there than you would be in the whitest neighborhood here. You may be black, but that's the only affinity you'll ever have with that continent. Blacks have a rich culture and heritage here, in this country. Why don't you want to know more about that instead of reaching out for something that will always be foreign to you?"

My comment was received with headshaking and scorn. "Africa will always be in our blood," he responded. "You're young. You don't know what you're talking about."

Knowing how I was viewed by my family and friends, I understood the additional unspoken message behind his words: "You don't like black folks anyway, so of course you want nothing to do with Africa."

I thought back to how I'd felt before my first visit to the continent—the sense of anticipation I'd had when I imagined that I was about to see the homeland, where I would finally be understood and accepted, a black man among black men. That fantasy had ended up being rudely shattered by the realities of the Ivory Coast, Liberia, Nigeria, and ██████. I didn't fit in there any more than I fit in back in America. It seemed I was truly a "white black man"—an anomaly and a misfit, no matter where my life's journey might lead.

# CHAPTER SEVEN

# American Dream Unraveling

F ROM THE FIRST MOMENT I'D JOINED THE AGENCY, I'D MADE
it known that I wanted to learn the most useful language for whatever foreign assignment I was given.

As you might assume, the various area divisions mandated that officers be able to speak a language relevant to their areas of responsibility, but this edict was rarely enforced. I was surprised at the number
of officers I met during my training days who spoke only English. I
learned that most case officers don't bother to learn foreign languages
because the conventional wisdom at the Agency is that language flu-
ency won't get you promoted—recruiting assets will. My unofficial
mentor, Ray, summed it up this way: "Having a language is a good
idea. It looks great in your performance appraisal, which of course
could help you get promoted. But, when you work as a case officer,
you'll find that most if not all of your targets speak English—especially
the people on the diplomatic circuit. So I wouldn't worry too much
about learning another language. The universal language of recruiting
agents is money."

Ray was echoing the general consensus of people at the Agency: that cold, hard cash is the most effective recruitment tool.

I was still determined to learn a language other than English. It just made sense to me. How can you understand what's going on in a country like Iran if you don't understand the language? I also felt I could bring something to intelligence operations in that part of the world that no white officer could. Like most people around the world, Iranians considered it obvious that black Americans were racially oppressed and would therefore share their revolutionary zeal. This meant that, as a black American who spoke Farsi, I could approach an Iranian feeling confident that my target would never dream that I worked for the CIA. What white case officer could plausibly discuss Malcolm X with an Iranian? I could—and I ended up doing just that, many times.

So I was pleased when, just prior to my last trip to Africa, I was slated to learn Farsi. The other two members of my case officer class who'd been selected to serve in NE division had some experience with Arabic. I'd noticed how difficult Arabic was when I tried to learn it on my own during my days at the Farm, and I was glad I would be studying a less complicated language. I hoped it would get me a field assignment that much sooner.

Even before starting formal language training, I taught myself the Persian alphabet and some basic terms. I also read everything I could find about Iran. I read the scholarly literature, the Koran, and Persian lyric poetry. I studied Persian history and began reading Iranian newspapers. The more I read, the more I realized that most of my colleagues at the Agency knew nothing about the place. Few people at the CIA could have told you that the Taj Mahal in India is a perfect example of Persian architecture. Few of them would have known who Omar Khayyam was or his significance in Persian literature. In fact, my colleagues expressed no interest in learning about Iranian society or culture, dismissing the entire country as a bunch of dangerous, foaming-at-the-mouth ragheads who would do anything for a few dollars.

I was glad to be learning Farsi for another reason. Language courses are taught in locations other than the headquarters at Langley, where I still had the feeling of being not so welcome. In this regard, I was far from unique. Many of the seasoned case officers I knew, including Ray, said they always dreaded returning to headquarters after working in the field. As Ray explained it, case officers in the field had the freedom to devise and run operations, while headquarters was a place dominated by "bullshit" forms and procedural requirements. Of course, as a black officer, I had different reasons for disliking headquarters—specifically, the subtle atmosphere of suspicion and alienation that surrounded me there.

For all these reasons, I was delighted to spend twelve months, starting in the summer of 1995, learning Farsi. My class was small in size and filled with both seasoned case officers and new ones like me, as well individuals from other areas of the Agency. It was good to find officers from the Directorate of Intelligence studying Farsi, since it seemed to me that the analytical side of the house needed language skills just as much as the operational side. And I enjoyed being a student again. I relished learning, and I had a particular fondness for learning new languages. My self-teaching served me well by giving me a basic familiarity with the language at the beginning of the class. I soon found that learning the language opened up a completely new and deeper understanding of what would be my target of prime interest as a case officer.

At the Agency language school, I was again in a situation where I was the only black person. However, I wasn't the only student of color. Taking Farsi with me was a new case officer by the name of "Manesh." I had never met anyone from India, and, after getting to know Manesh, I realized I still hadn't. To quote a line I heard in some nondescript movie or sitcom, Manesh came off as being "whiter than the whitest white man." A former US military officer, he seemed to take no pride in the fact that he had been born in India. In fact, he seemed embarrassed by it, especially when he interacted with the white officers in the class.

Being around Manesh made me reflect on my own situation. Was I just like Manesh, ashamed of my race? I hoped that the choices I'd made in life had nothing to do with an unconscious desire to escape the color of my skin. Eventually, a conversation convinced me that I was nothing like Manesh. For some reason, Manesh, like many other political conservatives, felt the need to explain to me what is best for black people in America.

"You know, Jeff," Manesh told me, "the best way for blacks to start off in this country is by joining the military." To back up his argument, he quoted a black military officer whom he'd heard on a talk radio show. I felt as if Manesh was chiding me for not doing the right thing as a black person in America. He was also subtly reaffirming an old belief that the only difficulties blacks face in this country are those they create themselves.

I felt compelled to push back. "Don't you think it's a pretty sad indictment of this country's racial attitudes if the only way a black man can get anywhere is by joining the military?"

"That's not what it means," Manesh responded, sounding defensive.

"Then what does it mean?" I demanded.

Manesh stumbled over his words, unable to come up with a reasonable response for his position. His opinion with regard to blacks was much like his opinion of his fellow Indians in America—they should do whatever it took to conform as upstanding citizens. Manesh fit right in with the conservative types who permeated the Agency. He and the five white officers in the Farsi class were devoted disciples of Reagan and were "ditto heads," the slang term used to describe fans of Rush Limbaugh. I think they were shocked to learn that, while I was from the same town as Limbaugh, I didn't describe it as a racially harmonious utopia the way he did.

A series of news events during my year of Farsi study brought out more of my classmates' extreme right-wing views. They were disgusted and horrified when the O. J. Simpson trial ended in an acquittal, and felt the unjust verdict by the predominantly black jury was evidently payback for the white cops who were acquitted of beating Rodney King back in 1992. They unquestioningly attributed the crash of a ValuJet airliner in May 1996 to the incompetence of the female pilot. And when the political campaign season heated up, they enthusiastically embraced the concept of "welfare reform," which Republican candidates were using as a weapon against the Democrats. Manesh even made a point of telling me about a mission he'd undertaken to see welfare abuse for himself. He and a friend had hung out in front of a welfare office and observed nothing but brand new Cadillacs parked by the building.

I couldn't let his assertion go unchallenged. "Manesh," I said as calmly as I could. "If what you say is true, how do you know that the cars belonged to the people in the welfare line?"

Clearly agitated, Manesh's voice became higher and he spoke faster, "Hey, we were sitting out there watching the people get into the cars."

"Uh-huh, sure," I responded. "Let me point out one thing to you. Can't you see how you are coloring welfare black by saying there were new Cadillacs parked in front of the welfare office? You're falling back on old stereotypes—namely that black folks are the ones on welfare and that they love Cadillacs. The fact is that a majority of welfare recipients are white people."

He could only say, "No, that's not it."

I'd heard enough, and quietly returned to my textbook.

It was okay that I didn't agree with my colleagues politically. Everyone can't think the same way, and I didn't fault them for their views. But our political differences became personal at the time of the Million Man March, the controversial black pride gathering organized by Nation of Islam leader Louis Farrakhan in October 1995.

Class was ending early that day, and I mentioned to my classmates that I was planning to go downtown and check out the march. Upon hearing this, the Reagan disciples jumped into action.

Disciple one, a seasoned case officer, asked in a very belligerent tone, "Do you support Farrakhan?"

"No, not on everything," I responded. "But I think this Million Man March is a good thing, and anyone who goes should not be automatically deemed a supporter of Farrakhan."

Manesh interjected, "You can't separate the message from the messenger!"

"Why can't you?" I asked. "Wouldn't you say it is a good idea for any man to renew his commitments to family, community, and personal responsibility? That is what the march is all about." I continued, "As for separating the message and the messenger, we all do that. I can't stand Ronald Reagan, but there were some things—not many, but some—that I could agree with him on. That doesn't make me a follower of Reagan."

Disciple two shook his head. "Well, in this case, I can't see any way to not consider you a supporter of Farrakhan if you're going to his march."

Disciple three then added, "You're going to let security know that you're going to the Million Man March, right?"

He was referring to a rule that requires Agency employees to notify and gain the approval of security prior to outside activities that may "expose the employee to hostile foreigners." I always strictly adhered to all regulations. I'd even filled out an outside activity request when I'd started coaching softball with Sandy. But this time was different. The Million Man March was nothing more than a large public event. Of course there were going to be foreigners there; people from all over the country were attending, and tourists from around the world would be present. By the same token, northern Virginia and Washington, DC, are always full of foreigners, and I never requested approval from security to walk down the street near them.

I answered, "No. I don't really see this as something that could have a security impact, so I don't think I need approval to attend."

Manesh demanded, "What if one of the television cameras shows you at the march? What are you going to do?"

"I'll wave, smile, and say 'Hi, Mom!'"

Given their reaction, you might have thought I was going to join the Black Panthers and start a revolution. They viewed my going to the Million Man March as a litmus test for my suitability to be in the Agency. It meant clearly that I was not one of them.

I don't know for sure whether any of the disciples reported my activity to security. Somehow I think they at least made it a point of conversation.

As for me, I don't really know why I was interested in attending the march. Maybe I was going as a sort of reaffirmation that I was black. All I know is that, when I emerged from the Smithsonian metro station adjacent to the National Mall, I felt swept up in a tremendous atmosphere of goodwill. There were smiles, hugs, and welcomes all around. I noticed nothing at all sinister about this gathering as I walked all about the Mall. I met people from California, Kansas, Mississippi, and many other states who had made the trek to Washington for the march. I was also happy to see groups of protesters who were upset about being excluded—rightfully, I believed—including women's groups and a group of Jewish men. It seemed that the gathering had far outgrown its origin as a Farrakhan-centered event.

I stayed for a couple hours and left just before Farrakhan took the podium. To be honest, though it was his march, he had nothing to say that I wanted to hear, and I didn't want anything to taint the good feelings I had absorbed. I wished the Reagan disciples from my Farsi class and the others I knew in the Agency had shared the experience. I know they would have been able to find something good in it.

Meanwhile, I was really taking my classes seriously. Some days I refused to speak anything other than Farsi, which I'm sure must have driven poor Sandy nuts. My language training continued through the huge snowstorm of 1996 and the government shutdown caused by a budget impasse. It was somewhat comical trying to explain to my neighbors, who believed I worked at some unidentified government agency, why I was going to work when the news was clearly showing government employees being turned away. "I'm just doing some studying at the library," I explained.

One day, I came home from class to find a surprise waiting: a wrapped present on the bed, addressed to me. For an instant, I panicked, worried that I'd somehow forgotten our anniversary. But when I opened the box, I found inside a softball outfit small enough for a baby.

With the box in my hand, I rushed downstairs to Sandy, who'd just come home from work. Despite the lump in my throat, I blurted out the words, "Does this mean what I think it means?"

Tears welling in her eyes, Sandy quietly replied, "Yes."

I caught her up in my arms and we stood there, embracing, both of us crying tears of joy.

I'd always worried about what kind of father I would be. I was fearful that I would be no better than my brothers, capable of providing the necessities but not of creating a complete family life—which, after all, was something I'd never experienced myself. But at the moment, all of those worries faded away. I knew I was going to be a great father. For possibly the first time in my life, I felt truly happy.

I was quite the proud father-to-be. The very next day, I went out and bought a copy of *What to Expect When You're Expecting*. In the weeks that followed, I read up on the Lamaze method of natural childbirth, health care and nutrition for mothers during pregnancy, breastfeeding, and many other topics. I dutifully accompanied Sandy to every doctor's appointment and usually asked more questions than she did. My attitude, as I often told her, was, "Your job is to have the baby, I'll take over from there." I was going to be the best damned father a child could have.

That pride must have been bubbling over when I told Miss Helen that Sandy was expecting. I really can't remember how she took the news, and at the time I didn't care. This baby was mine, and neither she nor anyone else in my family was going to have anything to do with it.

My elation came to an end a few days before Christmas 1995. The latest checkup seemed fine until the ultrasound, when the look on the doctor's face changed to a concerned frown. The routine visit turned into an intensive examination. Eventually, the doctor delivered the unthinkable news: the baby had not developed, and was not going to.

A sort of coldness seemed to envelop me. Sandy started to cry, and I reached over to hold her. The doctor gave us a little time alone to absorb the shock. Then she returned to present us with our options. She said that Sandy could just wait and naturally miscarry, or a procedure could be scheduled to end the pregnancy—a dilation and curettage, or D&C. We wanted to get this nightmare over with. The procedure was performed a couple days later.

That year, there was no holiday season for us. I took a few days off from language training to be with Sandy as much as possible. We cried a lot and did our best to comfort one another. After a time, we talked over what we'd been through, and we decided we would give pregnancy another try.

In the aftermath of Sandy's miscarriage, the two of us seemed to become closer than ever. I continued learning Farsi, tolerating the disciples by focusing single-mindedly on my studies. By the spring of 1996, Sandy was pregnant again. We were both cautiously optimistic, and I began dreaming about playing catch with my son or daughter one day in the not-too-distant future.

Several weeks later, in June, Sandy received a call from one of her sisters. Sandy's birth mother, "Louise," from whom Sandy had been separated for many years (she was divorced from Sandy's father), had been rushed to the hospital with complications from uterine cancer. Distraught, Sandy reached Louise on the phone. In an effort to renew her connection with Louise, Sandy told her what no one else in the family had been told—that she was pregnant. Still, Louise's health condition and the painful distance between the two of them left Sandy feeling sad and troubled, despite my best efforts to comfort her.

Sandy made plans to visit Louise around Independence Day, although I would be unable to accompany her because it coincided with my final exam in Farsi. As the time drew near, we didn't talk much about what she was feeling, but I could tell that Sandy was very nervous about reuniting with her mother.

During the last week of June, the medical checkup for the eleventh week of Sandy's pregnancy was scheduled. When the ultrasound revealed no signs of life, we were devastated for the second time. As the tears began to stream down Sandy's face, I sat there in shock and shame, feeling as though I'd let her down—as though somehow I was to blame for her miscarriages.

Two days later, Sandy went through another D&C. Two days of waiting for the procedure, two days of unanswered whys and painful silences.

Afterward, I was wondering whether we would or should try again, but it was too soon to raise the issue with Sandy. We both had other things on our minds. I had a crucial test to study for, and Sandy was about to travel for an emotionally complicated, probably painful meeting with her mother, whose condition, we now knew, was fatal. The drive to the airport was long and quiet. Little did I know when I left her at the gate that our lives were never to be the same again.

Even though my mind was on everything but Farsi, I managed to take and pass the test. I was scheduled to leave on an operational trip abroad on Monday, July 10. Meanwhile, I was hearing little from Sandy—an unusual experience, because we normally made a point of speaking by phone at least once a day whenever we were apart. This time, she didn't call me until a day before her flight home on Sunday, July 9. As we spoke, she wept and talked about the emotional exhaustion she was feeling, which seemed to explain the silence that had separated us.

I picked her up at the airport. We didn't talk much that evening. The next day, I left for work. When I returned home on Thursday, I took a taxi from the airport, knowing that Sandy was coaching a softball game.

When I got home, I noticed that Sandy's clothes were packed and some of her personal items were put away in a box on the bedroom floor. I didn't want to think about what was happening, so I simply waited for her to get home. After an agonizing three hours, she walked in, a softball bat in her hand.

"Sandy, what's going on?" I asked.

A terrible coldness in her voice, she said, "I don't want to be married anymore, Jeff. You need to be with someone who is going to love you as much as you love them."

I felt as if she'd hit me in the head with the bat. Trembling, I asked, "Why are you doing this? Are you just going to throw away the years we've spent together? We were trying to have a child together—now you just want to leave?"

I spent the rest of the night pleading with her to change her mind. She refused to sleep in the same bed as me that night, and the next day she did not return home from work. For hours, her mobile phone went unanswered. When I finally reached her that evening, she said, "I'm on my way to Atlantic City. I need to have a trip away and time to think things over."

She returned Sunday night and announced, "I've made up my mind to leave." Another tear-filled night followed, and the only tears were mine. I did everything I could to save our marriage. I begged her to reconsider, I proposed marriage counseling, I pleaded with her to tell me what I could do to make her happy. Nothing I said shook her resolve.

On Monday, I made the most difficult decision I'd ever made. "I don't want you to be unhappy," I told her. "I'm going to let you go. But I want you to promise that you will really think things over. And know that I will be here for you if you want to come back, no questions asked." I didn't know what else to do.

Sandy finished packing the car with her belongings, gave me one last hug, and left. I could see her crying as the car pulled away. I never saw her again.

In just a few days, so much that I had dreamed and worked for had just disappeared. In a little over a month, I'd lost a child and a wife. I took several days off from work trying to come to grips with what had happened.

Eventually, I gathered the strength to call my mother and tell her the news. My hand was shaking as I dialed her number. As soon as I said hello, Miss Helen could hear how upset I was.

"Sandy left me," I told her.

Almost immediately she said, "You see, that's what they do."

I was shocked at her response. It was as if she'd finally had the opportunity to tell me off for being with one of *them*—and it seemed she relished the moment.

I did my best to control the rage that flowed through me. "Thanks," I said. "That's just what I want to hear right now. Goodbye." I hung up the phone, not giving her the opportunity to say anything else. She'd said more than enough.

I spent days lying on the living room floor, staring up at the ceiling, feeling lifeless and lethargic. Eventually, I decided I'd experienced enough grief over what I had lost. With help from the employee assistance program at the Agency, I sought counseling for the healing that I so desperately needed. I felt a bit weak reaching out for help in that way, but it turned out to be one of the best things I ever did. Slowly I started regaining my focus on my work. I dedicated myself to it. I took time to learn more about Iranian politics and society, and to study problems like terrorism and the dangers posed by weapons of mass destruction.

As I continued my counseling and went through the legal process of being divorced from Sandy, I was advised that an overseas assignment was out of the question for the time being. Under the circumstances, I became a cubicle rat, just like so many others at the headquarters in Langley. I didn't mind the work, but the incessant conservative ramblings of the Reagan disciples who surrounded me continued to deepen my sense of isolation.

Here's a story that sums it all up. On November 6, 1996, the day after Bill Clinton was reelected as president, I just happened to wear a black shirt with a black pair of slacks. I didn't think anything of it until a woman in my office made a comment. "Judy" was a longtime administrative officer with the Agency, a white woman who happened to be the spouse of a case officer. "Are you dressed in black because Clinton was reelected?" she asked me. She assumed that, like the rest of the people in the office, I regarded the election of a Democrat as a cause for mourning.

I knew there was no point in engaging her directly. Instead, I smiled and replied, "Judy, don't you know? Black is not a color—it's an attitude!"

I heard a gasp or two from nearby cubicles, and Judy's face lost all of its color. Forcing a grin, she returned to her desk. My joke had confirmed to everyone in the office that I was definitely not part of the team.

My last tie to Sandy had been the softball team we coached together. It was a twelve-and-under team called the Redbirds, and Sandy had left in the middle of a season, not even bothering to say goodbye to the players. For weeks, they all asked where Sandy was. I came up with one excuse after another, hoping deep inside that she might eventually return. When the finality of her parting became inescapable, I gathered the team after practice and made the announcement that Sandy was gone and was not coming back. A couple of the players started crying. She was more than a coach to them—they looked up to her.

*She might have abandoned you, but I won't,* I decided. I offered to finish the rest of the season as the head coach, though I doubted I could do it. The season continued, and we all had a great time, even finishing higher than expected in the end-of-season tournament. Coaching those kids and watching them come together as a team helped lift me up from the devastation I'd experienced.

The divorce became final in February 1997. I learned from Sandy's stepmother that she'd married her ex-boyfriend and had a baby nine months later. It hurt to think about all that, but Sandy was no longer a part of my world. I was ready for the next phase of my life and prepared to finally take on an overseas assignment as a case officer. Now I was free to completely dedicate myself to the Agency—or, at least, so I thought.

# CHAPTER EIGHT

# Not White Like Them

I N THE AGENCY, IT IS CONSIDERED A HINDRANCE TO ONE'S CA-reer to gain exclusive expertise in any particular area. Case officers are supposed to be proficient generalists, essentially jacks-of-all-trades with skills that are transferable to wherever their talents are needed. During my extended time at headquarters, I was gaining specialized expertise in Iranian operations. I liked the subject area and enjoyed mastering it. But I was also realistic about what it meant for my career, and I knew that I would have to diversify in order to succeed at the Agency. Becoming an Iran expert would give me the opportunity to become familiar with other areas, such as rogue states, the proliferation of weapons of mass destruction, terrorism, and state support of terrorism. With knowledge and experience in these fields gained through working the Iranian challenge, I would be well positioned to transition to any other area of the Agency and thereby have a successful career.

With the drama of my divorce behind me, I was eager to go overseas. I was traveling operationally and doing just about everything else a case officer would do, but the successes I was having and the experience I was gaining were doing little for my career. A case officer based at headquarters can't possibly compete with a field officer when promotions are considered. So for my career to really go somewhere, I needed to go out into the field. However, for some reason, an overseas assignment was not forthcoming. I was an eligible case officer, perhaps more qualified than most because of my knowledge of Farsi, yet it seemed I had to constantly remind the personnel staff in NE division that I was ready for an assignment. After being overlooked repeatedly, I asked an official in the division when I was going to be considered for an assignment, only to be told that "everyone" thought I was still going through the divorce—though it wasn't clear who "everyone" was.

I found it interesting that my personal problem was viewed as so dramatic. As in any large organization, such problems are not unusual among members of the case officer corps. I met case officers who were going through divorce, substance abuse, investigation for alleged improprieties, and other difficulties. Nothing prevented these officers from receiving assignments, yet my divorce took me completely off the radar of those in charge of personnel decisions. I refused to take notice of the fact that, unlike those other officers, I was not white.

Finally the perfect position became available. A case officer based in a European country was moving on and a replacement was needed. Alongside the normal duties of a field case officer, he served as an expert on Iranian operations—an aspect of his work that I was more familiar with than anyone else, because I was his main point of contact at headquarters. I also felt that being based in a European country would be a valuable first tour in the field for me. As an important economic and political hub in Europe, this country would provide a multitude of operational opportunities beyond those solely focused on Iran. In addition, I'd previously spent time in Europe on successful operational trips and knew the lay of the land, particularly in regard to clandestine work, which I'd handled very effectively. No one I'd encountered during those trips had ever suspected me of being an officer for the CIA.

For all these reasons, I was the obvious choice as a replacement for the departing case officer. Nonetheless, I had to energetically lobby for the position. I must have been perceived as a pest because of how often I tried to sell myself as the most qualified person for the position; I mentioned it at every opportunity to NE division officials and to whomever else would listen. My lobbying finally paid off in January 1997, when I was formally approved to take the assignment.

I was excited to finally get the opportunity to show what I could do in the field. The country might not have been one of the hardship posts, like those in the Middle East or Africa, where just showing up looks good on a case officer's record, but I wasn't concerned with window-dressing my career. This was my first assignment overseas, and I was going to give it all I had.

I wasn't due to relocate there until late summer, so in the meantime I continued with ongoing operations and projects, which required several trips domestically and abroad. There were also a lot of boxes I would have to check before going overseas: fulfilling medical requirements, attending orientation sessions for first-tour officers, introducing myself to relevant headquarters area divisions that would be involved in my work, learning packing procedures, and more. I knew time would be tight, as I was still continuing to travel on shorter trips, but there was a whole cadre of administrative support staff at headquarters that I would be able to turn to as I made the transition overseas. I mapped out everything I would have to do, leaving nothing to chance. Having had so many things in my life that I thought were certainties change suddenly on me, I was the epitome of the doubting Missourian: I wasn't going to assume anything was real until you showed me.

My doubts were validated when I returned to headquarters after being away for a few days on an operational trip. Where before there'd been constant talk from some of my supervisors about my upcoming assignment and how well I would do, suddenly there was nothing.

I noticed people in the office avoiding me in the halls and averting their eyes when I walked into a meeting. It was obvious something was wrong.

After a few days of speculation, I walked down to my supervisor's office to ask what was going on. "John" was a veteran of many years and tours within the Agency, and an old hand at Iranian operations. He was a burly fellow with a thick mustache and cheery eyes. I had learned a lot from him about Iranian operations and respected his guidance. But that day, he did not seem his jovial self. After a few pleasantries, I blurted out my concern. "John, what's going on with my assignment?" I was within a couple of months of actually departing, and I wanted to know the facts.

John sat back in his chair, lowered his head, and without looking me in the eye said, "Well, we've decided to give the assignment to Peter."

I could barely get out the words. "Are you kidding me? He's not even a case officer."

Still avoiding my eyes, John said, "Well, he's got the language."

I waited for further explanation, but there was none. "Peter" had been detailed to NE division as an analyst from the Defense Intelligence Agency (DIA). Peter had near-fluent ability with the Farsi language, but he'd had no training or experience as an operations officer for either DIA or CIA. Having worked with Peter on various projects, I knew he was thinking about a permanent transition to the Agency, but I had no idea he was even being considered for any field assignment—let alone mine.

The whole thing made absolutely no sense. Though I didn't want to think it, Peter had just one characteristic that made him more qualified than me. He was white.

I thought that at least there was no way they would take an assignment away from me without giving me somewhere else to go. "So what is my assignment to be?" I asked John.

With a smile that any used-car salesman would envy, John said, "Oh, there'll be something coming along for you, don't worry."

I had been conditioned since childhood to understand that, when someone says "don't worry," that is exactly what you should do.

In a voice as composed as I could muster, I said, "Well, I would hope so." Then I added, "I think you're making a big mistake." With that single small gesture of rebellion, the meeting ended—and with it any hope for a meaningful assignment in Europe.

Over the next several weeks, I made an energetic search for another field assignment. Not finding anything suitable, I made an effort to create a position. As there was no field office in Iran nor any central hub for case officers with Iran expertise, it made sense for an overseas post to have at least one case officer who could undertake the position of referent or issue coordinator—an in-house Iran expert, if you will, who could enable the Agency to make useful connections with Iranians wherever they might be in the world. When NE division showed no interest in the idea, I shopped it around to other area divisions. I finally gained the interest of European division, which was willing to have me go to a different European post to serve as a case officer and Iranian referent.

The posting was to be in a country that was a hub of overseas Iranian activity. I personally undertook all the administrative work related to creating the position. By August 1997, I'd received the formal approval for me to go to the country as a case officer. Much as I would have been in my previously denied assignment, I was to be the in-house Iran expert, while also shouldering other duties suited for a first-tour officer. I was proud of the way I'd overcome my disappointment related to the canceled assignment and used it as motivation to find something else. The more I thought about working in this new country, the more excited I became about the opportunity.

I was going through all the preliminaries for the relocation when I was called to John's office on a Thursday afternoon. I went in feeling confident that I had taken care of everything and that there was nothing to prevent me from going to my assignment. I immediately knew that something was up when John offered me a seat and closed the door behind me.

"I don't know if you know it or not," John said, "but Peter won't be going to the assignment we had promised you." It had turned out that, two weeks prior to his arrival in the country, Peter had gotten cold feet and quit the Agency.

I could see what was coming next. Sure enough, John continued, "We feel that you are the most qualified for the position, and we'd like to you go in Peter's place."

I sat there in silence for a moment. Then, with a deep sense of satisfaction, I said firmly, "With all due respect, I have already been approved for an assignment. I'm going."

John looked up from his desk and said, "Oh, I know about that, but trust me, Peter's spot will be a much better position for you and your career." He continued, "We wouldn't offer you this job unless we knew you could handle it. You're a fine case officer, and I know you'll do the right thing."

I was being backed into a corner. With a bit of indignation, I replied, "Wait a minute. Before, I wasn't good enough to take the position, but now I am? Everyone knew it was a mistake to give the assignment to Peter, and now that he's quit, I'm suddenly good enough? You're offering it to me to save your butts, aren't you?"

Quietly but forcefully, I continued, "I'm sorry, but if I have to choose, I'm going to take the position I worked to create over the last couple of months."

John went on as if he hadn't really paid any attention to what I'd been saying. "Well, I want you to take your time and think about it, but we need to have something to tell the head of the division by the time he gets back." In other words, John was giving me twenty-four hours to accept their decision.

At John's suggestion, I took the rest of that day off "to think over what I was going to do." On the surface, they were offering me a choice, but I really had only one option. I spent that evening at home attempting to muster the nerve to stay firm with the original plan and refuse to go to the country they'd now decided to send me to. Just as I was gaining confidence in this strategy, the phone rang. "Bill" was a veteran case officer, currently in NE division, who was also working the Iranian target and with whom I'd worked on several projects.

"Hey, Jeff, what's going on, man?" he began. "You're going to take the position, right?"

I was shocked, having thought that no one else knew about my meeting with John that day. "Well, I haven't really decided yet, but I'm leaning toward not taking the new thing."

"Well, don't go pissin' the old man off," Bill said. He was referring to the head of NE division. "I'm pretty sure he'll want you to take the position, and it'll look good for you when promotion time rolls around."

After Bill's call, I received another call from another case officer in NE division, offering much the same advice. *They're ganging up on me*, I thought. Their plan was that I was to be their savior for the Peter fiasco, but I was having none of it. If I hadn't been sure about my decision before the calls, afterward there was no doubt in my mind that I was going to turn down the new offer.

I went to John's office first thing the next morning. "I've thought about it, and I'm going to stick with my original assignment," I said.

His face a blank mask, John simply said. "Okay. You'll have to discuss it with the head of the section."

The head of the Iranian section was a Senior Intelligence Service (SIS) officer who'd been appointed to the position by higher-ups, although many in the office—including me—had doubts about his knowledge of Iranian operations. "Adrian" welcomed me as I walked into his office.

I'd barely begun to take a seat when he remarked, "Jeff, I hear you've decided to go as planned for us."

A bit startled, I paused and looked up as I was sitting down. "Well, I did think about it," I replied, "and I've decided not to take the position. I have already been assigned, and I would prefer going there."

Clearly this was the first time Adrian had heard that I'd refused to accept the position. Tapping his pen, he gazed out of his office window for a few moments. Finally, he turned back to me. "Well, Jeff," he said, "you have to realize that the needs of the service come before the needs of individual officers. And right now, the service needs you to go to the position we've chosen for you."

I wasn't naive enough to accept that "needs of the service" crap out of hand. I explained to him all the benefits of the other European position, and showed why and how it was unfair to force me to switch as a quick fix for their mistake.

Adrian would have none of it. "Well, Jeff, you're going where we say," he declared, and turned to the papers on his desk with an air of finality.

It was clear that the decision had been made for me. It was where they wanted me or nowhere. I was directed back to John to go over the details related to the assignment.

When I returned to John's office this time, he had a bit of a smirk on his face, almost as if to say "I told you so." I learned then that the assignment I had worked for had been canceled almost immediately after Peter had quit. John went through a seemingly forced routine of telling me how noble I was to take the offered assignment and how great it was going to be for my career. In response, I tried to at least get some assurances. I attempted to make it clear that I did not want to be in an assignment with only one duty. I asked for nothing special—just to be placed like any other case officer, with a range of operational opportunities and decent support from headquarters.

Though John was looking at me while I was talking, I could tell he wasn't hearing a word I was saying. When he resumed praising my selflessness and calling me "the only person capable of taking this assignment," I couldn't help recalling a line from the movie *The Outlaw Josey Wales*. John Vernon's character is hearing a similar load of nonsense when he interrupts the speaker to declare, "There is another old saying, senator: Don't piss down my back and tell me it's raining."

It wasn't raining in John's office that day.

➤⬅

WHILE AT THE Farm, I had learned that one of the most important tools for a case officer is cover. Having the right cover is essential for a case officer to do the job. Most case officers go overseas with some sort of US government cover that will allow them ready access to individuals of interest to the national security of the United States. First-tour officers are normally outfitted with a US government cover. Having no cover at the beginning of your career as an officer with the CIA will jeopardize any potential covert career.

Cover, then, is crucial to the work and career of a field officer. Yet despite assurances made to me by John and other NE officials, I was sent to the field with a worthless cover. Rather than being given an official cover, I was saddled with a low-level administrative position little better than that of a janitor. Making matters worse, I knew nothing about my cover, and the Agency officials to whom I appealed refused to brief me on what to do with this cover and what operational opportunities would be available to me. The answer to my inquiries was always the same, "Don't worry about it." I was also told that my placement was out of their hands and there was nothing they could do about it; I had to take the cover that was available.

I traveled to the assignment in mid-September 1997, feeling apprehensive but determined to make the best of a less-than-ideal assignment.

On my arrival, I went to meet the CIA chief of the office. In the field, a CIA chief is essentially the king, almost godlike in his power—and often in his arrogance. The chief in this case was a classic example. As I sat quietly in his office, waiting to be acknowledged, he muddled around with some papers on his desk. Finally, after some initial pleasantries, he said, "Okay, as I understand it, you're here for one thing and one thing only—to finish managing the Iranian case you've already begun to work on back at headquarters." This was a case involving an Iranian national, living in Europe, who'd agreed to provide the Agency with information regarding activities by the Iranian government. Due to a change in his career status, this agent had actually lost most of his access to valuable information some time earlier, but we wanted to remain in touch with him. Having an actual living, breathing Iranian on our books as an Agency asset made us look good. So managing this contact would be my primary role.

Somewhat dumbstruck, I said, "That wasn't my understanding. I'm a first-tour officer. I'm supposed to be developing and using my skills, including devising, planning, and carrying out new operations. What sense would it make for me to be in the field doing only one thing?"

"Well, that's what the people from NE division told me when they were out here last week," he said. I was surprised to hear that people from headquarters had been visiting the office, and especially that they'd been discussing me and my career. The message they'd delivered to the chief was another indication that the assurances given to me by John and other NE officials—specifically, that I would be given a range of opportunities like other case officers—were basically worthless.

Trying not to come off as challenging or aggressive, I said, "I'm here to be a part of your team at this location. I want to be able to contribute like any other case officer posted here." As we continued talking, it was obvious he was more inclined to follow what the NE division officials had directed than to accept what seemed like common sense to me. This worried me. Having only one project in the field for a case officer is career suicide. At the beginning of my career, I had no desire to be stuck in a dead-end job. But I remained hopeful that this first assignment would give me the chance to prove my mettle as a case officer. I was eager to get started with my new duties.

The office was of medium size, with a staff of fewer than twenty, including case officers and support staff. As usual, mine was the only black face. As the in-house Iran expert, I had a lot of work to do on one long-standing, highly confidential project, but I was looking forward to branching out.

However, starting new projects or attempting to recruit new agents would prove to be almost impossible. Because I didn't have the proper cover or credentials, I was relegated to sitting back and watching the other case officers in action. And without the support of the CIA office chief, I had access to nothing beyond the single project

I'd brought with me. No one in the office seemed to take much notice of what I was doing. Meeting after meeting, while I sat and watched other officers receive operational leads and support, I was on my own. This was not turning out to be the kind of first tour I had expected and hoped for.

I did what I could to drum up business for myself. I attended any kind of social function I could find, from an art gallery opening to a get-together in a pub, where I suspected that individuals of interest to the CIA might be found. One such gathering involved young people in a government group having dinner at a local restaurant. I thought this might be a good group to infiltrate despite my less-than-desirable cover.

I ended up learning many lessons that night. The most important one was that working in Europe without speaking the native language doesn't make much sense. (I had wanted to take at least some introductory language classes, but John had assured me, "Everyone over there speaks English.") The dinner attendees did their best to talk with me in English, but their attempts were quite labored, and their words and facial expressions showed that they were puzzled by the idea that a US government representative could work overseas without knowing the local language.

One affable young staffer, "Joshua," approached me with curiosity. "You, um . . . you work with the Americans, yes?" he asked in broken English. "And . . . yes . . . What is . . . um . . . are your duties?"

I was never very comfortable with this question. "I'm a US government representative," was my standard response.

"And . . . yes. What does that mean? I mean . . . what do you . . . um . . . do?"

I pieced together a vague description of what I thought a janitor might do, but I could tell Joshua didn't buy it any more than I did. When he excused himself to join another group of people across the room, I was as relieved as he was.

I tried to take advantage of my overseas assignment by seeing as much of my new home as possible. I did my best to converse with anyone who would talk with me in the shopping areas, restaurants, and pubs. I found my new environs a very beautiful country, though it was hard for me not to think about the history of the place. Whenever I saw an elderly person, I wondered what he or she had been through in the past. There was so much I had learned about the history of the country, I couldn't help but be curious.

I encountered some surprising attitudes from the locals I met toward me as a black American. Over and over again, I heard admiring comments like, "We respect you so much for the struggles you've gone through" and "You've overcome so much in your country." I certainly felt that I received more respect as a black American here than I did in my own country, let alone within the CIA. However, this respect was reserved only for American blacks. African immigrants were detested by many as a sort of evil pestilence invading their land.

The other problem with my cover was ████████████████████ ████████████████████████████████████████████ ████████████████████████████████████████████ ████████████████████████████████, even if that cover is more robust and useful than mine.

On the other hand, it did provide me with the opportunity to travel the country for meetings with my in-country colleagues. I was obligated to confer with them on a regular basis, particularly as it related to the one covert operation I was permitted to pursue.

In November, having spent about two months in the assignment, I was scheduled for a short administrative trip back to the States. I was fed up with the situation. Though the office was controlled by EUR division, as the Iran expert, my operational tasking for the agent I was focused on managing was coming from NE division. Therefore, the office chief neither offered nor considered me for any work other than that which NE division dictated. This left me in the frustrating position of having to travel back across the Atlantic to find out what was going on with my career.

Back at headquarters, I requested a meeting with "Robert," who, as a manager in the Iran section, was partly responsible for my tasking as an Iran expert overseas. He agreed to the meeting, but to my surprise he specified that "Gerald," the counterintelligence chief, should be part of the meeting.

When the meeting began, I jumped right to the point. "Why aren't I receiving any assignments? And why was the office told that I'm there for one thing and one thing only?"

Robert glanced at Gerald, then said, "Well, Jeff, you know, you kinda stick out as a big black guy speaking Farsi. We think you might draw unwanted attention back to the one project you have there."

I could only ask the first thing that came to my mind: "Tell me, when did you first realize I was black?"

My sarcasm was greeted with a moment of silence. Then Robert replied, "Well, we've discussed this with Adrian and others, and they agree with us. It's a matter of security for you and your operation." He tried to make it sound as if the decision to not use me was for my own good. But I wasn't buying it.

"So what you're telling me is that I was truly sent to the field to do only one thing."

"Yes, for the moment. It's about security." Then they moved on to offer me assurances that, in time, I would be fully engaged as a case officer in the field—but only on cases that would be operationally secure for me. And since the color of my skin was not going to change, neither would the range of opportunities available to me.

I ended up proposing my own solution. "Well, if things don't improve for me out there, there really is no need for me to stay. I can manage my one project from here." The meeting ended and I flew back.

I began to wonder whether I should consider myself a victim of racial discrimination, and perhaps even threaten legal action against the Agency on that basis. I didn't know whether I had the right to make such a claim, and I viscerally shied away from blaming my career problems on my skin color. After all, I'd spent my whole life trying to rise above the attitudes of ignorant people who wanted to pigeonhole me because of my appearance. But the thought that what I was dealing with at the Agency was racially driven was unavoidable. After five years, I'd never heard of any place where a white officer was deemed unable to operate effectively because he sticks out due to his skin color. The fact that most of the case officers in the Africa stations were white attested to the fact that only black officers were made to suffer career limitations due to their skin color.

I returned with no idea of what was going to happen. I wasn't willing to wait very long to find out.

After another month, nothing changed; I still only had the one project, and I was basically prevented from doing anything else. I was a case officer, but I was not being treated like one. In December 1997, I informed the head of the field office and officials of NE division that I was departing. This was a drastic step. One of the few acts that can seriously tarnish a case officer is returning from an assignment short of tour. By returning way short of tour, I would have to face a sort of exile from the ranks of case officers in good standing.

Agency management said nothing to me when I announced my decision, but NE division made veiled threats to charge me for the moving expenses I'd be incurring because I hadn't stayed in the field for a year. I responded by saying that I would fight any decision to penalize me for standing up for myself. Though somewhat veiled, it was the first reference I'd made to the possibility of filing a complaint regarding my treatment. In response, NE division quickly acquiesced, allowing me to return "at the convenience of the government," which meant I didn't have to pay for my journey home from abroad.

When I went back to work in Langley, I found that I was more isolated than ever. It was as if my posting to the field and all my accomplishments had never happened. No one would talk to me about it except the few black officers I knew. All of them, especially my friend Henderson, were unsurprised by what had happened and in fact viewed it as typical. When we discussed my experiences, I seemed to hear an echo of my mother's words after Sandy left me: "You see, that's what they do."

I happened to run into the officer who had been chosen to replace me in the position I left. Like me, "Victor" had a background in Iranian operations. When we started to talk, I felt a vague need to apologize to him, wondering how he'd been affected by the mess I'd been in. But that feeling quickly faded. When I asked Victor how he was dealing with the cover issue, he told me he'd been given a full US government official cover without ever having to ask for it.

Of course, Victor was white.

I considered leaving the Agency, but a complex combination of feelings led me to reject that possibility. Years of feeling rootless and alienated wherever I went had fueled a deep desire to find someplace I could call my own. Five years earlier, I'd focused that desire on the Agency. I still had hopes that I could find a home there. After all, the Agency is large, with many departments and niches—surely there was one where my skills and personal qualities would be welcome. What's more, I felt I owed it to the mission of the organization to give the place another chance. I'd trained for over two years to become a case officer, and I wasn't going to just throw it away. I wanted to demonstrate—to others, and to myself—that I could rise above the petty ignorance that I faced and even overcome the tarnished status I now seemed to have. More than ever, I had something to prove.

In January 1998, I accepted an assignment in the counterproliferation division. This was the only part of the Agency that would take me on, despite my qualifications and years of experience. I was happy to get away from NE division and gain experience in another part of the Agency. My work for CP division provided an opportunity for me to make use of the knowledge I'd gathered in managing the Iranian target, and I found the new assignment a welcome change. But after a few months, I once again began feeling the urge to go out into the field. I filed application after application for positions I was clearly qualified for based on the job descriptions and requirements. Time and time again, I was turned down. The reason was always the same: because of my working status in a previous posting, I was ineligible for other positions suitable to a clandestine officer such as myself.

I understood the logic behind this rule—although I couldn't help noticing the fact that many exceptions seemed to exist. I'd known several case officers, including John and Robert, who had taken onward positions after having a working status similar to what I had had in the field. Of course, those officers had something I didn't have: white skin.

However, I still refused to accept the notion that the color of my skin explained the setbacks in my career. I wanted to blame something else—bad management, inefficiency, anything but racism. The only thing that was crystal clear was that I was unable to escape the damage done to me by NE division.

In late 1998, I was close to giving up on my dream of a lifelong career in the Agency when an opportunity finally came along. A good friend by the name of "Carl," who worked domestically for the Agency's NR division, told me about a position in his division. Like me, Carl was experienced in Iranian operations; in fact, we'd worked together a number of times. Carl suggested I would be a perfect fit in New York. While this wasn't an overseas assignment, it was the closest domestic equivalent available within the Agency. The job was offered to me, and I accepted it.

As I made arrangements to move to New York, I found my old feeling of excitement about the Agency coming back. This new assignment might give me the chance to get back into the mix of things, showing everyone that I was capable of being an effective field case officer. I was ready for a fresh chapter in my CIA career, and I hoped it would open up a promising new future.

# CHAPTER NINE

# New Beginning, Same America

I WAS DUE TO ARRIVE IN NEW YORK JUST AFTER CHRISTMAS. Since this was the fourth time I'd been relocated in the last two years, I had the routine pretty much committed to memory. I had already found an apartment and was just finishing some last-minute preparations at headquarters prior to my departure. One bitterly cold day, made even worse by a very strong and unforgiving wind, I had just parked my car and was making my way to the headquarters building when I felt a strange sensation in my chest, as if bubbles were popping in and around my heart. By the time I reached my desk, the feeling had grown in intensity and my left side was starting to feel tingly. I tried to ignore the discomfort, but after an hour it had gotten so bad that I made my way to the office of medical services. As I waited for the nurse to finish a phone call, a wave of numbness came over me. I staggered back, my chest tightened, and my vision went black.

"Are you all right?" the nurse exclaimed.

"Uh . . . no. Something's going on with my heart."

The moment I mentioned my heart, the nurse sprang up from the desk and reached for my wrist. Within a moment or two, she rushed me to one of the examination rooms. The next thing I knew, after an EKG and the insertion of a painful IV in my hand, I was being wheeled on a stretcher to an ambulance bound for the nearest hospital.

At the hospital, I was attached to a monitor and given another EKG. The nurse examining my readings looked worried. "So, you're not in any pain?" she asked.

"Not really, just a nagging discomfort in my chest." My answer seemed to surprise her.

I was told I had an irregular heartbeat, and I was given medication that was supposed to fix the problem. But after about two hours, one of the doctors told me, "The medicine is having no effect. We'll have to admit you."

A routine morning had morphed into an ordeal that would last four days. Rather than ringing in the new year in the Big Apple, I found myself watching Dick Clark celebrate on the TV in my hospital room, wondering what had happened to me.

In a funny way, I found my stay in the hospital interesting. All the patients around me seemed to be at least thirty years older than me, which probably helps to explain why I quickly became a favorite of the nurses. One of the nurses who came to chat with me had been born in Iran, which gave me the chance to speak Farsi during my stay. My main worry was whether my condition—whatever it was—might derail my New York assignment. A few colleagues from CP division came by to visit, but there was no talk about my assignment, and I heard not a word from any Agency officials.

As for my health, I was baffled. I worked out regularly, had a relatively healthy diet, and had no history of heart problems. The discomfort I was feeling did not seem serious enough for the attention I was receiving—yet, periodically, the nurses would rush to my room to ask if I was feeling okay, apparently responding to a spike on the monitor.

Finally, one morning, a doctor paid me a visit to report their findings. "The blood tests are showing an injury to the heart," he explained.

"Does that mean I had a heart attack?"

"That's right," he said. He also mentioned that I'd had a severe reaction to the medications they were giving me. The night before, my heart had either slowed down or stopped a couple of times. I had only a hazy memory of the nurse coming in to check my blood pressure and then rushing out to get a doctor. Finally, the doctor told me, "Given the erratic nature of your heart rhythms, you're also in danger of having a stroke."

All of this came as a shock to me. A week before, I'd considered myself a healthy young man. Now I didn't know whether I would get out of the hospital alive.

My nerves were shaken further when a nurse mentioned that, if nothing else worked, they'd have to use shock treatment to "get me back to normal." "They'll just give you a few thousand volts, no big deal," she remarked off-handedly.

"No big deal?" I said. "Have you ever had a few thousand volts sent through *your* body?" I was picturing the way Jack Nicholson looked after the shock treatments in *One Flew over the Cuckoo's Nest*. She just smiled and continued taking my blood pressure.

Thankfully, on the day the shock treatment was scheduled to begin, my heart rhythms suddenly normalized.

Only after I left the hospital did the seriousness of what I had just gone through really hit me. My apparent near-death experience redoubled my desire to move forward and put all the past pain, struggles, and disappointment behind me. I was looking forward to moving to New York and beginning the next phase of my life.

Nothing could have prepared me for what I had in store. My first reaction to New York City was to be thoroughly intimidated by everything I saw, from the majestically tall buildings to the incredible numbers of people everywhere. But within days the feeling of intimidation turned to wonder. I began to feed off the energy and vitality of the city. There was so much of everything: cultures, foods, smells, sights, sounds, something to impact all the senses. I wanted to see, touch, and experience everything. My apartment was in midtown Manhattan bordering on two neighborhoods: the theater district, home to the Broadway shows, and a residential community formerly known as Hell's Kitchen but recently rechristened Clinton (I liked the sound of the old name a lot better). I spent hours getting lost on the subway, learning my way around, and walking through the city's many neighborhoods: the Upper West Side, Harlem, Alphabet City, the Village, Tribeca, SoHo, and more. I made a point of visiting the outer boroughs that tourists rarely see—the Bronx, Brooklyn, and Queens—giving short shrift only to Staten Island, a sparsely populated suburban enclave that didn't really feel like part of New York City at all.

For me, the most inviting aspect about the city was its diversity. New York is a microcosm not just of the United States but of the world—it is a place so vast and varied that it scarcely seems to matter what group or race any individual might belong to. I wasn't delusional; I knew that the differences between black and white still mattered. After all, I was still in America. But in New York, I felt no pressure to be black, or white, for that matter. I could gladly just be another faceless, nameless individual, free to be myself without feeling forced into any particular category. For the first time in my life, I felt at home.

However, I was in New York not as a tourist but to work for the Agency, and I was eager to get going. An Agency case officer based in a domestic city such as New York has duties largely similar to those of an overseas case officer: mainly finding and recruiting spies. There are a few differences. Domestically based case officers may do more nontraditional operations, they may engage in greater contact with domestic companies in order to gather business-related intelligence information, and they have more contact with the FBI. Otherwise, the work of a domestic case officer is very much the same as that of a foreign-based officer—particularly when it comes to the importance of cover. On day one, I met with my direct supervisor. "Dick" was a longtime Agency veteran, a pudgy guy, and an avid baseball fan—his office was filled with Yankees paraphernalia. I would come to learn that he was a font of tall tales about his exploits as a case officer, though they were rarely related to actually recruiting anyone.

It was important to me that Dick understood the seriousness of my work ethic. "I want you to know that I'm here to make the best contribution I can to this office," I told him.

"Now that's what we like to hear," Dick responded. "I heard you had some problems in the field, but I want you to know that that won't have any impact on you here." I wasn't surprised to learn that the rumor mill had been at work with my story—and I was worried that the version Dick had heard had been one-sided. But I brushed off the concern and pressed ahead.

Most new case officers need time to get started, but I hit the ground running. I brought a number of Iran-related cases with me, and I'd actually started working on them even before arriving in New York. I was also eager to get going on my own projects, especially non-Iranian ones. I told Dick all about the cases I had and my plans for them. He listened politely, then changed the subject as soon as he had the chance.

"Those cases you have are fine, but get out there and get me some scalps, and I'll get you promoted," he said, using Agency-speak for recruiting new spies.

"I mean no disrespect," I replied, "but I'm not here looking to get promoted. I'm here to do the best job I can. If I get a promotion out of it, so much the better."

Dick looked a little confused; I don't think he'd ever heard a new case officer speak about his job in quite the same terms. But I felt it was important for me to explain the new perspective I'd gained as a result of my brush with death. "I don't know if you heard or not, but I just came out of a situation where I didn't know whether I was going to live or die. That made me do a lot of reflecting about my life and my work. What I've realized is that the most important thing for me is to do a good job. That's why I'm not worried about only doing those things that will get me promoted." Dick just nodded, seeming uncertain as to how to react.

Next, it was time for me to meet with the head of the office. Although "Jerry" had never worked as a case officer himself, he was now in charge of the CIA's New York office. Like Dick, Jerry was uninterested in the cases I brought; he, too, emphasized the promise of a promotion if I brought him a bunch of good recruits. He liked to describe the operational area of New York as being "no bigger than Dulles airport," implying that, for him, the city included only a few select parts of Manhattan and therefore should be a compact, easy place for any case officer to manage.

I found it hard to take Jerry's advice on operations seriously, especially when I realized that he didn't know basic procedures, such as how to secure the office at the end of the day. Over time, I realized that he'd taken the New York job as a kind of retirement tour, using most of his days to network with corporate types in an effort to line up a high-paying job as soon as he left the Agency.

Dick and Jerry were like a lot of Agency veterans in emphasizing the quantity of recruits that an officer collects rather than their quality. They emphasized that New York was a great place to be—it's overflowing with foreigners who live and work in the city. But the more time I spent in New York, the more I questioned whether the many foreigners I encountered had access to information important to the national security of the United States. I began to wonder whether playing the numbers game, as most Agency professionals wanted to do, really made much sense as a counterespionage technique.

I had another problem with producing the kind of results that Dick and Jerry were looking for. Even if I'd been wholeheartedly committed to playing the numbers game, I didn't have the tools to join in. Once again, it was a matter of my inadequate cover.

Prior to arriving in New York, I'd made several inquiries about what cover would be available. As far as I knew, I was still strapped with the same worthless cover I had previously . The answer was always the same: "Don't worry. Take care of it when you get there." But now that I was in the city, I was told that there was nothing they could do about it. I had no choice but to try to get by using the same cover I'd been saddled with before.

The cases I had didn't involve any sexy foreign contacts. However, they did provide some valuable information related to economic security. I was enthusiastic to start work on my own cases, and they turned out to be very labor intensive and I did a good job with them. Lacking the proper cover, I used my own initiative to gain access to potential agents. For example, I went to a number of cultural events where I eventually made contact with several individuals of interest, including one Russian national who'd been highly sought-after by the Agency. When I told Dick that the Russian had responded to my inquiries with a positive return message, he looked surprised and impressed. "That's the first time we ever got a Russian to call back," he said.

"Well, if I was able to establish contact without even having the proper cover, imagine what I could do if I had it." Dick shrugged and walked away.

I also had success with a highly restricted project known as Operation Merlin, one of several operations for which I won acclaim from headquarters. "Merlin" was the code name for a different Russian national, one I was introduced to as a ████████ (although he denied this characterization). Because of his background in engineering, Merlin had been recruited to serve as a conduit to Iranian scientists. The plan was to feed him designs for a component part of a nuclear weapon that he would, in turn, pass along—in exchange for pay and access—to the Iranians. The catch: the designs were deliberately crafted by scientists at ██████ National Laboratories to include technical flaws. This meant that, if the designs were implemented, they could set back the Iranian effort to build a nuclear device by a number of years.

For about two years, I was the case officer in charge of managing our connection with Merlin—despite the fact that I was warned from the start that he had a less-than-favorable view of black people. Having dealt with such attitudes for a quite a while, my only reaction was, "It'll be okay." I was not going to let such narrow-mindedness hinder me in my work. As far as I could tell, I was able to manage Merlin effectively throughout our relationship. It required a lot of tact and hand-holding; he was very nervous about being involved in international intrigue, and there were times when only his greed kept him from bailing out altogether. But I kept him hooked throughout the lengthy, delicate process.

Though Operation Merlin was my most important case, it wasn't my only one. I was repeatedly ranked first or second in my branch for reporting information considered valuable for national security. I was doing all I could to build my portfolio of accomplishments as a case officer.

One of my most important achievements was helping to improve the Agency's relationship with the local FBI agents. Turf wars—in which the CIA proclaims supremacy over foreign operations while the FBI claims control over the United States—often create mistrust when a CIA case officer is working domestically or an FBI agent is working abroad. During my training, I continually heard Agency veterans berating the FBI as a bunch of glorified cops who knew nothing about intelligence operations. I imagine that FBI agents must have felt similar dislike for CIA case officers. But I knew I needed a good relationship with the FBI while working in New York—after all, I was on their turf and they were a great and necessary resource. So I organized operational planning meetings with FBI agents, and established a working dialogue with them. Showing them respect for their work helped me earn their respect for mine. The resulting cooperative relationship proved beneficial for both sides.

Unfortunately, my contributions didn't impress my superiors. I was constantly hounded for not bringing in any new business. Dick even threatened to terminate all of my Iranian cases, saying they were taking too much of my time and preventing me from being able to bring in new cases.

"Yes, the Iranian cases are keeping me busy," I told him. "But my lousy cover won't let me get access to the kind of people you want me to contact. Why not provide me with something better?" He ignored my request.

Eventually, a pattern emerged in the behavior of management toward me. They took steps to make it appear as if they were providing me with the same operational opportunities as everyone else. For example, I repeatedly received notice of ████████ gatherings that might provide a good forum for an officer to get some scalps. How could I claim unfair treatment if the record showed that I was given these leads? The only problem was that, without the proper cover, I was unable to attend such events. There were even times when I showed up at events only to be turned away because I had no credentials. (Fortunately, I was never arrested for trying to gain entry to official functions.) The closest I could have gotten to any diplomat in New York would be visiting the UN as a tourist.

Every time Dick threatened to send me home if I didn't turn it around, I requested the same cover that every other officer had. The answer was always the same: "Nothing can be done." There were other instances of unfair treatment. My accounting, unlike that of my peers, was always double- or triple-checked, every operational decision I made was questioned, and my operational initiatives for new business were consistently quashed. Meanwhile, the only other case officer at my level was treated solicitously and provided with support and mentoring.

I wasn't surprised when I heard through the grapevine that complaints had been lodged against Dick regarding his tolerance of a "hostile work environment" for women and minorities. I hadn't been one of those making a complaint, but I was glad to know that others were speaking up.

One small but painful example of the differential treatment I received occurred during the weeks before New Year's Day 2000, when there was widespread fear that glitches might make the computer system vulnerable to attacks by hackers and terrorists. In response, management throughout the Agency put out a call for volunteers to man the offices over the upcoming Y2K weekend. I'll never forget the day volunteers were requested at a New York branch meeting. I wanted to do all I could to be considered a part of the office, so I was eager to volunteer. But it turned out that I was the only case officer to do so. The meeting was adjourned, and we were told that a decision about time slots for the duty would be announced the next day.

The next day, when I asked what time slot I was supposed to man, I was told, "Well, since no one volunteered, we decided to assign officers ourselves."

I felt deeply hurt. The day before, a roomful of officers had witnessed me raising my hand to volunteer, yet I was told to my face that "no one volunteered." It was getting harder and harder for me to avoid the feeling that I was not wanted as a case officer in New York—and maybe not anywhere in the Agency.

As the months went by, my sense of alienation and loneliness at work continued to grow. Seeking out a place of refuge, I spent most of my lunch hours in the courtyard of the World Trade Center. I was always fascinated by those twin towers majestically shooting up to the sky. I didn't care that I looked like a typical tourist gaping skyward as I admired them. There were free concerts during the spring and summer, and I always had a good time watching the throngs of people enjoying the music or just hanging out.

Sometimes I would go to the courtyard just to think things through. Considering what was happening with my work, I could sense that my days at the Agency were numbered. I was giving up on the notion that I could somehow get a fair shake, whether because of my skin color or for some other, hard-to-fathom reason. I needed to take steps to ensure my ability to weather the coming storm.

I decided to take the New York bar exam. If I passed, it might open up some new career opportunities for me. For instance, I might be able to work for the CIA's Office of General Counsel after my current tour came to an end.

Just after Christmas 1999, I started a three-month bar review course. I attended class from 6 to 10 p.m. every night during the week, though I had to miss several classes when work demands extended into the evening. It was tough to regain my old mastery of the complexities of law after so many years away from legal practice. I wasn't feeling very confident as the mid-February date for the two-day bar exam approached.

In the meantime, the pressure from my supervisors kept intensifying. They scheduled repeated meetings with me about my performance while continuing to deny my requests for the cover I needed to do the job. I proposed a series of ideas for new operations, only to have them tossed aside by my New York supervisors. I continued doing my job with what I had to work with, but it was becoming increasingly clear that I was being set up for failure.

Despite the pressure from management, I continued making strides with Merlin, as our plan to feed him flawed nuclear designs evolved. But a turning point arrived during the winter of 2000, when a meeting in a California hotel was arranged between the scientists from ███ National Labs and Merlin to review the plans that were to be presented to the Iranians. I was there, along with "Bob," the Agency manager who was directing the project.

The scheme was a complicated one. As Merlin understood it, we were handing him incomplete plans for nuclear weapons that he would be authorized to sell to the Iranian scientists. These plans alone would not enable Iran to build a working bomb. But they would be valuable enough to entice the Iranians into a longer-term relationship with Merlin—during which we would coach him in techniques for eliciting inside knowledge about the Iranian nuclear program. Thus, under the pretense of providing information to the Iranians, using the partial plans as bait, Merlin would actually be gathering information, which he would ultimately share with us, his American friends. Merlin's reward: cash payments from both sides in this complex dance of deception.

What Merlin didn't know was that we'd built an extra layer of trickery into the scheme: namely, the design flaws that would make the partial plans we were providing unusable.

I'm no nuclear scientist, so I didn't understand much about the plans themselves. That wasn't my role. During the meeting, my intention was to focus on Merlin himself, to make sure he continued to be comfortable with his role as the conduit for the top-secret information. I watched his facial expressions, his body language, and his other reactions to make sure he was feeling okay about the operation as it entered this crucial late stage.

But when Merlin was handed the plans for the first time, I was shocked at his reaction. After just a brief look, he said, in his accented English, "This won't work."

I was alarmed at what I heard. Not wanting to cause a scene, I immediately pulled Bob aside. "This is a big problem," I said. "If he is able to see the flaw, don't you think the Iranians will too? And if they can tell that the plans are fake—"

Bob cut me off. "Don't worry about it," he said. I found this response less than comforting.

I left the meeting with a very uneasy feeling about the entire operation. It appeared to me that the scheme the Agency had developed was too clever by half—that the obviousness of the design flaws would quickly expose the fact that Merlin was working for the CIA and render the whole operation worse than useless. Later, I would repeatedly question Bob about what had happened, only to have my concerns brushed aside. I described those concerns in my written reports about the project as well.

No one ever spoke to me about the potential problems with Operation Merlin, but from that moment on, things only seemed to get more strained for me at the Agency. The situation came to a head on April 6, 2000. I was summoned to Jerry's office, where I found him waiting for me with two other members of management, his deputy "Charlie" and Dick's replacement, "Henry." Despite the complaints against him for creating a hostile work environment, Dick had been promoted.

No one would look me in the eye as I sat down. Jerry started the meeting by saying he was very disappointed with my failure to bring in new business. He supported his critique by citing statistics from a departmental database that listed spy recruitments by case officers. No information was included regarding the quality of recruits or the value of the information gathered. This was the numbers game I'd dreaded.

The other officers chimed in with derogatory statements about my work as a case officer. Charlie said, "One would think you were here just to take advantage of the situation"—in other words, to enjoy the perks that came with living in Manhattan. Though he was a new-comer to the office, Henry joined in as well, saying that I'd "been given opportunities, but didn't take advantage of them." I spoke up in my own defense, reminding them that I'd been a consistently good reporter, that the high-level cases I brought had been going well, that I'd made great strides ███████████████████ and even with Operation Merlin (despite my concerns about it), and that I'd worked effectively with the FBI. It all fell on deaf ears. It only got worse when I mentioned the fact that I was the only officer without decent cover; they all seemed to roll their eyes, as if to say, "Here he goes again with the cover thing."

My trial having concluded with a verdict of guilty, Jerry then pronounced my sentence. "You'll be receiving a new tasking in a day or so. If you don't fulfill it in every detail over the next two months, you'll be out—sent back to headquarters."

"Okay," I responded. "When I see the new marching orders, I'll consider what you're offering and I'll let you know what I think."

I received the tasking later that day from Henry. In the next two months, I'd be required to recruit three different people, each with operational approval from headquarters and the relevant field offices, and to have at least three meetings with each one.

I'd spent enough time in the field to appreciate the complexity of what they were demanding. The fact is that this new tasking required me to do something that no case officer would be able to accomplish in a year, let alone two months, even with the appropriate cover.

I couldn't just accept this unreasonable assignment. Jerry had left the office for the day, so I went into Charlie's office and requested two things: an additional month and the cover I needed to accomplish the tasking.

Charlie's response was a simple no. "You've had ample opportunity to do the job, and you're not doing it."

I protested the disparate treatment and demanded to know the reasoning.

"I'm not getting into a debate with you," he said.

I made an effort to remain calm. "Other officers have the cover that you've been refusing to give to me. And since you're claiming that I've been failing to deliver on the job, I can think of one officer in particular whose statistics were also poor. In his case, you not only gave him the proper cover, you also gave him a full year to turn it around." I fell silent for a moment. Then I continued, "I would like you to explain why you are treating me so differently."

Without looking at me and with a wave of his hand, Charlie said, "I don't have to explain anything."

A powerful sensation of pent-up energy exploded through me. I'd had enough.

I stood up and said, "You're treating me differently than everyone else, and you're completely disregarding the contribution that I've made to this office. You're setting me up to fail. If you intend to send me back to headquarters, so be it. But understand that I will be taking the necessary steps to protect myself." I walked out of his office.

I immediately set about investigating the process for filing an Equal Employment Opportunity Commission (EEOC) complaint based on racial discrimination.

I learned that, because I worked for the federal government, I was required to exhaust all internal procedures prior to initiating any court action. I had my doubts about the ability of the Agency to conduct a fair and objective investigation; scuttlebutt from veterans like Henderson and others I'd spoken with had told me that the Agency routinely dismissed discrimination complaints or sabotaged them through a review process that was sharply skewed in favor of management. But I realized that I had no choice but to follow the prescribed process. Because there was no real structure in the field for filing a discrimination complaint, I had to deal directly with the EEOC office at headquarters.

I knew I was facing a tremendous battle. I'd learned in law school and from observation that complaining about discrimination exposes a black person to harsh, even vicious attacks. It's curious; virtually all Americans agree that racial discrimination is wrong, but few white Americans actually believe anyone who complains about it. No other legal action in this country—except perhaps a charge of sexual harass-ment or assault—places the victim on trial quite the way a claim of racial discrimination does.

The prospect of filing a discrimination complaint troubled me for another, more personal reason. In a strange way, I found myself wondering whether I even had the right to file such a complaint. My childhood and early life experiences had left me alienated from my family and from the black community as a whole. I'd tried to live a life beyond race, which had made the people I'd grown up with dismiss me as someone who was trying to be white. Now I was in the odd position of claiming blackness as a way of demanding the justice I felt was due to me. Did this make sense? Was I claiming to be black while having no intention of actually identifying myself as black? Was I even black enough to claim racial discrimination?

Agonizing over the issue, I came to a realization. It was not a ques-tion of how black I was. What I felt about myself had nothing to do with what I'd experienced in the Agency. It was the Agency that was making an issue of my race, by allowing the color of my skin to define how my bosses treated me. There was no doubt in my mind that their actions toward me were wrong. I was ready to stand up for myself—as a black man, and especially as a black American.

Over the next couple of weeks, I worked on wrapping up my cases. I wanted to make sure that the work and projects I had started didn't suffer unnecessarily. Unfortunately, there wasn't much I could do to guarantee their success. For example, my departure meant I would never know for sure what was happening with Operation Merlin, and whether my fears about the plan potentially backfiring would turn into reality. But that couldn't be helped.

In mid-April, I traveled to headquarters to formally request a new assignment, though in my heart I knew it would be a futile gesture. My career with the Agency was over.

While at headquarters, I also asked for a meeting with the deputy director of operations to discuss my case. I was a bit surprised when he agreed to meet with me. On April 21, Good Friday, I went to his office. "Tom" was a middle-aged man with silvery gray hair and eyes that looked almost worn out, as if they had seen a lot in life. We were joined in his office by his executive assistant and the chief of personnel for the Agency—three white managers across the table from me, the lone black person.

At Tom's invitation, I described my experiences in New York as well as the questionable treatment I'd received throughout my career. When I mentioned how I'd been told, "You kinda stick out as a big black guy," I could see a collective wince from the three managers. They listened patiently and politely, taking a note or two.

Then it was Tom's turn to speak. "It's our goal at the Agency to maintain a work environment free of discrimination," he said. "I personally have no tolerance for any behavior that is unfair or biased." The meeting concluded with Tom's promise to look into the matter and a request that I "hold off for a while before I do anything."

I felt some sense of satisfaction about being able to state my position. In particular, the meeting left me with the deep realization that what had happened to me was not a matter of one or two isolated occurrences but rather the reality of my life as a black case officer in the CIA.

I finally realized that the environment at the Agency is suffused with the assumption that the managers, who are almost exclusively white males, are obviously superior to the handful of minority-group members who happen to find their way there. Those white managers are willing to tolerate the presence of minorities, so long as they know their place.

I'd refused to accept the race-based limitations that I'd experienced as a black person growing up in Cape Girardeau. Now I had to resist the same kinds of shackles at the Agency—even though it meant girding myself for the fight of my life.

# CHAPTER TEN

# Man Without a Country

THE OFFICE OF THE DEPUTY DIRECTOR OF OPERATIONS SENT A representative to meet with me, in an effort to defuse the situation. "Russell Campbell's" card described him as special assistant to the director for diversity plans and programs. He was a black retiree who'd been personally invited by the director of the CIA at the time, George Tenet, to return and run the Agency's diversity program. He was a pudgy fellow with salt-and-pepper hair, a scraggly mustache, and a pair of bewildered-looking eyes. He'd been in the Agency for a long time, so I figured he had some idea of the difficulties black people have to face there. I didn't expect him to believe what I was claiming out of hand, but I did expect a sympathetic and understanding ear.

I traveled down to headquarters on May 1, 2000, to meet with Russell in his office. After I described what had been going on in my career and particularly the recent events in New York, Russell told me, "This office was created to eliminate the subtle sort of discrimination that it appears you have experienced."

"Subtle?" I said. If Russell considered my experiences subtle, I had to wonder what he thought of as blatant.

He then asked me who my mentor was in the Agency. It's typical for new recruits to have a veteran officer as a sort of sage, lending support and guidance for ascending the career ladder, but I'd never enjoyed that kind of relationship. The only veteran officer who'd expressed any interest in my career development had been Ray, who had retired by the time I became certified as an operations officer. This was an echo of my entire life. As a boy and young man, I'd never had a mentor in black America to tell me what was right or wrong, where I belonged, and what I needed to do in order to succeed. I told Russell that I'd never had a mentor at CIA.

"Well, that's unfortunate," he said, in a way that made it sound like merely an administrative oversight.

We talked for a bit longer, and then he said, "The director asked me to meet with you to see what I could do to make you happy." This was the problem. Russell had no real interest in my discrimination complaints. Where I wanted to confront the issue head on, he only wanted to make a bad situation go away. He even went on to affirm that, when a person joins the Agency, he "gives up his civil rights." As an American citizen, I couldn't fathom the idea of losing my civil rights—especially not as a result of becoming an employee of an agency supposedly dedicated to protecting freedom. Given the gulf between our perspectives, there was little he could do to appease me.

Russell and I met a few more times. When we talked, he offered generalized lamentations about my circumstances, mingled with praise for what he considered the progressive racial policies of the CIA. Whether these remarks were sincere or mere fodder to placate me was difficult to determine. After a while, I grew tired of the feeling that he was in contact with me only in order to keep an eye on me for management, and I let our relationship lapse.

Many people committed to racial equality in America have advocated the idea of forcing change from within. The idea is that black people who can get a foot in the door can pave the way for others to make the same journey. Russell had his opportunity to do this. After all, he'd been personally asked to assume a position of authority with regard to racial sensitivity at the Agency. Yet because he was content to be a mouthpiece for management, he became more of a hindrance than a force for change—a mere insurance policy for the status quo. I often wondered how Russell felt about himself, not only as a black man but simply as a man.

If Russell Campbell was one face of the CIA's reaction to my challenge, another would present itself shortly. When I returned to New York in early May, I had quite a surprise waiting for me: a notice, dated May 3, 2000, that I was scheduled for updated security processing.

When I'd joined the CIA, I'd had an initial security processing, which involved a full background check as well as a polygraph test. Then I worked for a three-year trial period, after which I was required to pass another round of security processing in order to become a full-status employee. Full-status employees are scheduled to undergo updated security processing every five years. This is the kind of security check that was noted as being negligent in the case of Aldrich Ames, the KGB double agent.

The security updating process is lengthy and very labor intensive, which is one reason that the Agency's security office is generally behind schedule when it comes to administering these checks. And while it is technically true that any employee can be randomly selected for updated security processing at any time, it's exceedingly rare for an employee to have an early security update.

I'd completed and passed my trial-period security processing in 1997, which meant I was not due for an update until at least 2002. This notice was more than two years early. I refused to view it as a coincidence, especially considering the fact that the notice had arrived almost immediately after I made my discrimination claims.

Security processing, and particularly the polygraph test, is used by the CIA to intimidate recalcitrant employees, especially minorities. When an employee complains about being treated unfairly, he or she is automatically scheduled for the polygraph. After the test has been administered, the employee is told that there are "questionable readings" with regard to such matters as unreported contact with foreigners or, even more damaging, unreported contact with hostile intelligence services. The actual test results are never shown to the employee. Instead, the mere report of negative results is used to badger the employee with threats, including the removal of security clearances, firing, and—worst of all—an FBI investigation. The experience usually ends with the employee mired in a career-ending security process or making a false confession simply to escape the ordeal.

I'd heard rumors of this technique throughout my years at the Agency, and I'd recently witnessed it firsthand when one of my training classmates filed a gender discrimination suit. Until now, I'd always convinced myself I could never be one of the victims. Now I could see that I was being set up for the full treatment, and I refused to submit to it. I called and left documented messages for both Russell Campbell and the deputy director of operations' executive assistant, telling them that I would not believe the timing of my early security processing update was coincidence and stating my refusal to submit.

Agency regulations say that refusal to submit to a polygraph test when so ordered is an offense warranting immediate dismissal. However, I was never contacted by security about my refusal. No one had anything to say about my complaint regarding the "coincidental" decision to demand an early security update from me.

Meanwhile, the process of adjudicating my EEOC complaint was underway. During one of my trips to headquarters, I met with the NE deputy chief, "Chris," and the NR division chief, "Nancy." The latter was a woman who'd been thrust into a management position not because of her skills as a case officer, but simply because she was in the right place at the right time. The lawsuit by women case officers had resulted in a $990,000 settlement in federal court in 1995. In response, the Agency was taking women like Nancy and giving them highly visible positions.

Like Russell, Chris and Nancy tried to appease the angry black man by asking where they could put me in the Directorate of Operations.

I told them that I would prefer finding a position outside of the DO—and that in any case I planned on continuing my EEOC action.

Nancy replied, "Well, Jeff, I don't know everything that happened in your last assignment, but Jerry says that there is and has always been a place for you in New York."

She looked at me as if she expected me to be pleased, but that was the last possible response. I was so angry, I could barely choke out a few words: "He said that? After—" I was unable to continue. I was thinking about how Jerry had refused me any support, ignored my accomplishments, set me up to fail with a series of impossible demands—all effectively pushing me out of his office. And now he was saying that I would always have a place in New York.

In the most calm and quiet voice I could muster, I finally replied, "The best thing for me is to return to New York and finish closing out my cases." With that, the meeting was over.

The Agency's EEOC office began negotiations with me for a possible settlement. Unfortunately, the proposals they made were laughably inadequate. They started with an offer of $5,000 in return for my resigning and relinquishing all claims and actions against the Agency. After I rejected that offer, they responded with one of $10,000. Evidently my career wasn't worth much to them. My goal wasn't some kind of a windfall. But I wanted a settlement that would adequately represent the seriousness of the unfair treatment I'd received at the hands of the Agency, as well as a sum of money sufficient to help me get started in a new career.

By the end of April, the only thing on my mind was the developing situation with the CIA and the looming end of my career. I was in my New York office when I received a call from a classmate from the bar review course, a nice young woman with whom I'd developed a casual friendship.

"Jeffrey," she said. "I was wondering if you knew the results were coming out tonight."

"Results? What results?"

"Didn't you know that the bar exam results are going to be posted online at midnight tonight?"

"What?!" I blurted. I had completely forgotten about the test. We agreed to meet for dinner and a movie prior to taking a look at the results together, although given the recent trajectory of my life, I wasn't feeling very optimistic about my chances.

The evening turned into a much-needed diversion from the tension I was grappling with. We went to a theater that specialized in classic films to watch *Casablanca*, one of my all-time favorite movies. As I watched, I pictured myself as a modern-day Rick Blaine, a man without a country, forced to be a loner but able to survive and willing to fight the good fight.

Close to midnight, my friend and I parted company, as neither of us could stand the thought of looking at bad news together. She decided to go to her office while I made my way to my apartment, just a couple of blocks away. I was reluctant to check out the test results, so I walked around the block two or three times until I finally got up the courage to go home.

The first thing I noticed was a blinking light on my telephone answering machine. When I pushed the button, I heard my friend's voice: "Oh my God! Jeffrey, you passed! I passed! I'm so happy!" I let out a thunderous "all right!" that must have awakened several of my neighbors. I spent the next several minutes running back and forth and jumping up and down in my apartment. Despite it all, I'd done it—I'd passed the New York bar exam. Now I had somewhere to go, something to take me beyond the anger and disgust I was experiencing with the CIA.

By late August 2000, I'd completed closing out my cases. I was ready to leave New York and return to headquarters at Langley, where I'd wait to learn the results of my EEOC complaint and the final stages of my fading career at the Agency.

During my last week in New York, I attended my final staff meeting. It was a forgettable meeting until a new group of case officers was

introduced. Henry welcomed them on behalf of the team and then announced, "We'll get you set up as soon as possible with US ████████
cover so you can go after the prized guys out there." I couldn't believe
he had the nerve to say that with me in the room. The very thing I'd
been repeatedly denied was being handed to these new white officers
on their first day. That was the clearest message possible that I didn't
belong and wasn't wanted.

The last night in my apartment was very somber. The movers had
already taken my possessions and the place was completely empty. I
couldn't get over the feeling that I was being forced to leave the one
place that felt like home to me. White America was throwing me out,
casting me aside for no reason I could comprehend. I had no idea
where I was going or what was in store for me. I was facing an unknown future but still believed that there was something out there that
was better than what I was going through.

On the first day of my return to Langley, I was called before the
NE division security officer. He handed me an envelope containing
another notification that I had to submit to an updated security processing. "Thanks," I said. "I'll file this one with the other one." They
were still coming at me, and I was still fighting.

I got a lot of curious glances and awkward silences from my colleagues at headquarters. Everyone knew something bad was going
on—for the second time, I was returning before the end of my tour.
When I reported to NE division, I was offered a couple of do-nothing
desk officer jobs, with no potential for any sort of promotion or career
enhancement. Their plan was to put me out to pasture.

I refused the positions and opted to find something within the
Agency on my own. I raised the possibility of working in the Office
of General Counsel, but in response, management attempted to make
the position part of a settlement: in return for them letting me serve as
an attorney in the Agency, they demanded that I relinquish all claims. I
didn't think that accepting a job assignment—a perfectly normal, mu-
tually beneficial action—should require me to drop my discrimination
complaint. That took the General Counsel job off the table.

After some searching, I found a position in the recruiting division, which I thought would offer me the perfect opportunity to make a meaningful contribution to the Agency's efforts to recruit minorities. I knew I could set aside any hard feelings, be professional, and help bring about a future that I still deeply believed in: an Agency that represented all Americans. I made my pitch for the position with the head of recruiting during a meeting in early September 2000, and she tentatively agreed to take me on. But there was a catch: before I could take the job, I would have to be released by the DO and NE divisions.

That catch proved fatal. DO and NE division officials refused to permit me to take the position in recruiting, though no one from either division told me of their decision. Two months after I'd spoken with the head of recruiting, Russell Campbell told me that management didn't think I would be able to "adequately represent the interests of the Agency in such a position."

It was clear that I was definitely persona non grata at the Agency. People would give me a wide berth as they passed me in the hallways; no one would look me in the eye. Even the black employees, while sympathetic to what I was going through, chose to keep me at arm's length. I understood their behavior—any close contact with me could have put them at risk for the lash. They were providing me with the best support they could under the circumstances.

For a time, I didn't even have a desk until they decided to put me in a windowless office no bigger than some of the holding cells I remembered from my days at the public defender's office. After a few days, I was joined there by my classmate who was filing a gender discrimination suit, and we spent many weeks together in the room that we dubbed "the penalty box."

Finally, in December 2000, I was summoned to the office of Chris, the NE deputy chief. He said that since I had not found nor attempted to find an onward assignment, I was being directed to return to my previous office within NE division. I pointed out to Chris that I had found positions but that the division had refused to release me. He said he knew nothing about that and directed me to report to the office by the next week.

"You want me to go back to the office that considered me 'too big and black' to get assignments?" I asked.

He said, "We don't know anything about that. Anyway, that was a while ago. Management in that office has changed, so you won't have to worry about anything like that." He at least had the decency to admit that the problem had been real.

"I have to ask you one more question." I said. I'd tried long enough to reason with these people. Now they were going to hear me and answer my questions. "There is still the issue of my updated security processing. I haven't heard a word from anyone about my refusal to submit to it. By your own regulations, I should be fired for refusing. I would think you want that addressed before sending me to work in what is one of the most crucial accounts in the Agency."

Chris hesitated briefly before responding, "As far as we know, security has discussed the matter. It will be dealt with once your EEOC case is over." I had never heard of such a procedure and certainly had heard nothing from security.

"Well," I said, "I don't think it will be in my best interests to report to that office. I would like some sort of response on the positions that I have found."

"If you refuse to report," Chris said, "we will have to initiate procedures to terminate your employment."

"Do what you feel you have to do, but I will not report to that office." I got up and left. It would be another two and a half months before I heard from management again.

→←

WITH ALL THAT was happening to me, it occurred to me that, as an American citizen, I ought to reach out to Congress. I wasn't expecting the politicians to offer me assistance with my legal battle, but I thought they would at least like to know what was going on in the CIA with regard to the treatment of minorities. And I hoped that attention from someone on Capitol Hill might at least ensure that I would not fall victim to any heavy-handed tactics the Agency might attempt.

My first step was to contact the House and Senate Intelligence Committees. While there was no reply from the Senate, the House did respond, and I made several trips to Congress to meet with staffers from the House Intelligence Committee. I was optimistic about the potential of these connections until I realized that my main contact, one of the staff attorneys for the committee, had formerly worked for the Agency's Office of General Counsel. It became apparent that she viewed her job as running interference for the Agency. She praised "the changing face of the Agency" and repeatedly told me, "I'm sure you'll be afforded a thorough investigation as to your claims."

During one of my meetings with this woman—who happened to be black, by the way—we were startled when the ranking Democrat member of the committee walked into the room. He was a congressman from California named Julian Dixon—a black man. I spent the next hour and a half talking with him about what was going on with me and the overall situation with black people at the Agency. He expressed his disgust and said that he was going to look into the matter personally. I eagerly granted his request to be able to look over my personnel records. As the meeting ended, I felt comforted that at least someone with some clout was going to take an interest in my situation.

Within a couple of days, I got a call from Russell Campbell asking if it was okay for my personnel records to be made available to the House Intelligence Committee. I agreed, of course, although I wondered how he and other Agency officials were going to spin the situation to Congressman Dixon. But I was hopeful.

When I heard nothing over the next few weeks, I decided to call the staff attorney to ask for an update on Congressman Dixon's inquiries. There was a long silence. Finally, the attorney spoke. "Oh, Mr. Sterling," she said hesitantly. "I'm afraid we've lost the congressman."

"What do you mean? Did he lose reelection or something?"

"No, no," she said. "The congressman died of a heart attack during a trip home."

"What, he's dead?" I said. "You have got to be kidding me."

"No, we're all pretty shaken about it around here. I thought you would have known."

This latest twist in the story was one of the weirdest. I'd met the congressman just a few weeks earlier, and now the poor man was dead. I wasn't surprised that the staff attorney made no offer to refer my situation to Congressman Dixon's replacement. His sudden death provided a perfect opportunity for her to bury the whole matter. That was the end of my effort to solicit help with my discrimination case from Congress.

On March 1, 2001, I received notice from the Agency that I was being placed on administrative leave. I was required to report to an outbuilding where I had to surrender my badge and all documentation from the Agency. While on administrative leave, I was not allowed to enter any Agency building or to have contact with any Agency employee with regard to Agency business. I was to call in to the office that handled those on administrative leave every day between 8 and 10 a.m. Were I to miss calling in even once, I would immediately be placed on leave without pay. Finally, I was informed that I was to remain on administrative leave pending the outcome of a panel being convened to review the suitability of my continued employment with the Agency.

I was shown the paperwork related to the charges against me that were to be examined by the panel. It said that I was being placed on administrative leave for "insubordination" and that an item to be considered was my refusal to "look for or accept an onward assignment." Most shocking, the next section said that I would have only one level of appeal regarding the panel's decision because I was a "trial employee." A trial employee? After eight and a half years of service?

Of course, I protested this absurd misstatement of facts, pointing out that I had successfully completed my trial period by passing updated security processing along with every other requirement. In response, it was decided that I would be given a second level of appeal. When I asked the administrator, "Does this mean I'm recognized as a full-status staff employee?" I was told, "No, it means you are a post-trial-period employee just for this process."

"This is ridiculous," I protested, "What kind of sense does it make for me to still be considered a trial employee?"

"Well, look at it this way," she said. "This isn't really hurting you. In fact, it's giving you another level of appeal. And besides, a lot of employees have the same sort of situation. Some have been trial-period employees for most of their career." I suppose it might make sense to someone steeped in bureaucracy, but it didn't make any sense to me.

Before I left, she had one more piece of news about my employment situation. "By the way, your cover has been removed retroactive to your entrance on duty."

"Wait a minute!" I said. "Do you mean to tell me that, before a decision is made, my cover is taken away? Doesn't that make it pretty automatic that they are going to fire me?"

"Oh no," she said. "You still have your two levels of review."

I was shocked. This meant that, for all intents and purposes, I had never been undercover. My immediate thought was concern for those I had had contact with during my work as a clandestine case officer for the CIA.

I assumed that I'd receive some kind of security briefing to tell me how to handle this dramatic reversal of status. I wanted to know things like areas to avoid and steps I should take for protection. But nothing like that was in the cards. The administrator handed me a fax number for employment verification. "That's all," she said.

On another day, later in the process, I requested to see my security file and my personnel file, wanting to make sure there were no erroneous entries. The Agency requires that a security officer be present when any employee reviews his or her own security file. I was allowed to take notes, but I had to use a pen and notepad provided by the security officer.

Under the watchful eye of the officer, I opened my file and took immediate notice of the first entry, a document detailing my security processing history. It noted successful security processing at entrance on duty and after the three-year trial period, then noted that I was not scheduled to undergo updated security processing until 2002.

As calmly as I could, I asked the officer, "If I'm scheduled for security updating, even if it is random, shouldn't that be noted in this security file?"

"Yes, anything to do with security processing should be noted there in your file."

"Thank you, that's all I wanted to know." This was strong evidence that the May 2000 demand for an updated security process had not been a coincidental or random request but rather retaliation on the part of the Agency. But who was going to believe me?

I continued to leaf through the file, taking notes. But I was mindful that the notepad had been provided by the officer. An old trick I'd learned at the Farm was to discover the thoughts of a contact by looking at the pages underneath those he or she had written on. To avoid being victimized by this obvious ploy, I wrote in Farsi, and then removed several additional pages below the ones I'd written on before returning the notepad to the officer. If security was interested in what sort of notes I was taking, they were going to have to find out another way; I had been trained well.

As for my personnel file, there was nothing in it other than preliminary items from when I joined the organization, including a few glowing performance appraisals that didn't reflect the position I currently found myself in. It was as if I had never been a part of the CIA, as if my career was nothing but a lie.

My main takeaway from the departure process was a feeling of deep sadness. Eight and a half years had come down to this. Piece by piece, everything that I had earned and worked for had been stripped away. Once, I could walk proudly into any Agency building; now I had to have permission and subject myself to a thorough search.

I grew more and more angry at how I had been treated by the Agency, and more determined to make a fight of it. I contacted lawyer after lawyer, pleading my case and requesting assistance. Each lawyer acknowledged my problem, saying, "Everyone knows that there is racism at the CIA." But they refused to get involved. No one wanted to take on the CIA, especially since I couldn't deliver a class-action suit—there simply weren't enough black officers at the CIA to qualify for certification as a class.

I even turned to the NAACP Legal Defense Fund to seek assistance. The call was eerily similar to the one I'd made so many years ago to the United Negro College Fund. The director whose name I'd been given was sympathetic but told me, "We don't normally take on such cases unless you have a class of people you can bring forward. I'm sorry, but give us a call should you get other employees who are interested in joining you."

As the days passed, I sank into a deep depression. Friends had abandoned me, perhaps fearful of guilt by association; no one wanted to be seen with the idiot who was fighting the CIA. I couldn't turn to my family for help. I'd never told them that I was in the CIA, and if they'd known, they would have believed I was now suffering because of my own mistakes—especially my rejection of my family. All I could imagine was my mother repeating, "You see, that's what they do," over and over again, perhaps relishing the punishment I was suffering for fleeing to white America. Black America didn't want me, and now white America had tossed me out.

My feelings were exacerbated in early 2001 when the final result of the EEOC investigation was released. The report sided completely with management, disregarding the numerous affidavits I'd provided that verified my claims of discrimination and documented my record of achievement. Instead, it colored me as a failed employee, almost a failed experiment. I knew it was just a matter of time before I was fired. Sure enough, in May 2001, I learned that the panel had decided to terminate my employment with the Agency, and my first appeal with the executive director failed as well.

Feeling increasingly isolated and purposeless, I found myself having that recurring nightmare from my boyhood once again: the dream in which I am a tiny, helpless being trying to escape from some looming, evil presence that is pursuing me across a vast, dark, and dangerous landscape. Every time I had the dream, I would wake up in a cold sweat, my heart pounding, and I was often sobbing with a sense of complete hopelessness. My real-life world and my nightmare world now seemed to be converging. I began seeing a therapist, finding at least a modicum of relief in being able to talk about my suffering with a sympathetic professional. But those moments of comfort quickly gave way to renewed feelings of despair and misery.

I was still bitterly angry about the one-sided EEOC investigation. The bastards had won, and it seemed there was nothing I could do about it. But something made me want to keep fighting back. My case kept getting turned down by attorneys once they realized I couldn't come up with a few thousand dollars as a retainer. The clock was ticking and the deadline for filing was approaching fast. Eventually, my anger and frustration turned to resolve. I decided that if I couldn't find an attorney, I would sue the Agency on my own. After all, I was a licensed attorney and I knew my way around a courtroom.

The old saying has it that any lawyer who represents himself has a fool for a client. That might have been true in my case—but my client was a determined fool.

I was scared to death at the prospect of suing the Agency without representation, but I had come this far, and I saw no reason to back down now. Writing and preparing the filing was easier than I thought it would be. It seemed I still had some lawyer left in me.

In late August 2001, I traveled to New York to file my lawsuit against the CIA. It felt strange and a little disturbing to be back in New York as a visitor and not a resident. It was only the second time I had visited the city since my forced departure a year earlier. My other visit had been in October 2000, when I was sworn in to the New York bar—a day of immense pride for me. I felt no less proud on the day I filed my suit against the CIA, my first action as a duly licensed attorney.

I felt charged up after I filed those papers. I had no idea what the outcome was going to be, but I knew I was doing what felt like the right thing. I had always been a fighter, and now the CIA was going to find out how much fight I had in me.

But after filing the suit, I found myself wondering, *Now what? Where was I to go, and what was I to do?* I had no idea. Everything I had tried up to that point in my life had been a disaster. Had I made the wrong decisions, chosen the wrong paths, opted for the wrong America? I hadn't found myself in white America; maybe there was something in my past—in the black America that my family represented to me and that I thought I'd rejected forever—that could help me understand who I was, why I'd had to undertake my painful journey, and what my future might bring.

The answer came to me without my having to look for it.

# CHAPTER ELEVEN

# The Death of Hope

WHENEVER I GET A CALL FROM HOME, I AUTOMATICALLY ASsume the worst—a death, a serious accident, something like that. It's a natural assumption to make; after all, I rarely receive a call from Cape Girardeau with any happy news. It was no different when my mother called in early December 2001. The news was that my father was in a bad way. He was in the hospital in Los Angeles, maybe with cancer.

My immediate reaction was to say, "Why should I care? He's no father to me." But I stopped myself and regained my composure. I continued, "Well, maybe I'll give him a call." My mother gave me the number of the hospital, and our conversation was over.

As I thought about it afterward, I decided there was no way I was going to waste my time calling him. He'd been completely absent from my life, so what reason did I have to care that he was dying? Yet over the next couple of days, the image of the man in a hospital room was all I could think about.

I realized I had to call him, though to this day I can't really explain why. Maybe there was a part of me that wanted to be a good son, even to a man I didn't know and who'd done nothing to nurture, guide, or support me. I was accustomed to being in one-way love relationships that gave me a feeling of duty and obligation, even though my respect and affection never seemed to be returned. Perhaps my connection with my father was just the latest example.

It took several calls to the hospital before I was finally able to reach the man my mother called Howard. Whenever I'd spoken to him in the past, he'd had a strong presence on the phone. But this time, his voice was noticeably weak and frail, almost to the point of being unrecognizable.

"Howard, is that you? This is Jeff."

He seemed surprised and pleased to hear from me. As we talked, I could hear some sort of mechanical humming in the background, the kind of sound you only hear in a hospital. I asked about his condition.

In a voice barely more than a whisper, interrupted by wheezes and coughs, he said, "Well, the doctors say it's cancer, but they caught it in time. All I have to do is undergo some procedures, and everything will be fine."

With a bit of a tremble in my voice, I said, "I will come to visit if you want."

Chuckling, he said, "Well, it's been how many years? Yes, I would like it very much if you come to visit." He'd said things like that before, and I'd always shrugged them off. But this time was different. This time he was dying.

The description he'd given of his condition sounded reassuring, but I wanted to hear something from his doctor directly. I managed to reach him by phone after a few days. "I'm sorry, but Howard has pancreatic cancer," he told me.

"I understand, doctor," I said. "But he told me that it was caught in time and that he was to undergo treatment."

After a pause, the doctor replied, "Is that what he said? I suppose he doesn't grasp the reality of the situation. Or perhaps he just doesn't want to. Pancreatic cancer is treatable if it's caught in time. But in this case, it has already spread to Howard's liver."

"Does that mean his condition is inoperable?"

In a matter-of-fact tone that suggested years of experience in delivering bad news, he said, "Yes, it is inoperable. There is not much we can really do for him at this stage other than make him comfortable. It's possible that, with chemotherapy, he might live another six months. I've been suggesting admittance to a convalescence home, but Howard wants nothing to do with that. I'll be talking to him again tomorrow."

I didn't know what to feel about having it finally confirmed that my father was dying.

I called Howard the next day. His voice sounded a bit stronger and I could sense a change in his outlook. "Were you able to speak with your doctor today?" I asked.

"Yes, I did, and he told me what was going on. He told me I'd have to start chemo next week once they let me out of here."

I was glad to think that maybe he was finally accepting what was going on. "Well, Helen told me that Mark was on his way out to LA, so he'll be there to help you out."

Evidently, my calling my mother by her first name did not sit too well with him. "That's no way to talk about your mother," he remarked. "When you come out here, we are going to have a long talk, and I will tell you everything you want to know. But regardless, remember that she is your mother. And I am your father."

It was almost as if he knew what was on my mind. Since our last conversation, I'd been thinking about the idea of visiting him, and I'd begun to feel excited about our finally having a chance to talk. I had so many questions that only he could answer—about him, about our family, about me.

My brother Mark arrived in LA by the end of the week. I spoke with him on the phone. He told me he'd flown there because he'd heard about Howard's refusal to be admitted to a home. "He can't take care of himself anymore," Mark said. "He's wasting away, Jeff. He looks pretty bad."

Howard was due to start chemotherapy on the following Monday. When I called Mark to find out how the treatment had gone, he told me, "He refused to go. I think he just wants to die."

"I'm going to try and come out in the next couple of weeks," I said.

"I don't think he's going to make it that long, Jeff," Mark said.

Sensing the urgency in Mark's voice, I called him on Wednesday to say I'd made arrangements to fly out that weekend.

"I'm glad you're coming, Jeff," Mark said. "His pain is really bad. In fact, it got so bad he decided to let them do the chemo like his doctor said. Not a nice way for a man to spend his birthday."

Of course, I'd had no idea that it was his birthday. In fact, there was very little I really knew about my father. He had never been anything to me but an occasional voice on the phone. Once during my college years, he'd made a visit to Cape. I'd heard that he was there from my mother just before I was due to arrive home for Christmas vacation. I was full of anticipation during the bus ride. What would he be like? How would we get along? I was finally going to find out—or so I thought.

But when I got home, I found a house full of angry people, the living room a mess of shattered furniture, my mother in tears, and my father nowhere to be found. Little by little, my mother told me what had happened. Howard had told Mark that he was not his father, that my mother had been with another man and had never told Mark the truth. Mark became enraged, confronted my mother, and took out some of his anger on the sofa and chairs.

My brother Michael offered to take me to meet Howard at the hotel where he was staying, but I turned him down. Having seen my father's handiwork, I didn't want to meet him.

Years later, while planning a trip on Agency business to the Los Angeles area, I decided to visit Howard. I called him and said, "I would like to come see you. Do you want to see me?"

"Of course I would like to see you—I'm your father. I'm so glad that you want to come for a visit."

I had arrived in Los Angeles around 11 p.m. I picked up my rental car and immediately headed over to Howard's place, on South Flower Street in the middle of South Central LA. I was expecting burned-out buildings and streets strewn with junk; instead I found an avenue lined with palm trees and cute little two-story apartment buildings with charming Mexican facades. But when I buzzed my father's apartment using the intercom system, there was no response—although I'd told him clearly in advance when I'd be arriving. Thinking he might have stepped out for a moment, I sat in my car, watching and waiting. After an hour and a half, I gave up and drove to my hotel.

During my week in LA, I called Howard's number and left a message every day. He never called back.

When I got home, I described what had happened to Mark, who was living in LA by then. "I wonder if Howard was out of town," I said.

"No, he was in LA all week," Mark assured me.

But that was years ago. This time, I felt confident that nothing would prevent me from seeing my father. As I stared out the airplane window, the questions I wanted to ask him kept revolving in my head: "Did you ever care about me? Did you not want to have anything to do with me? Was I a bad son or a disappointment to you? Why didn't you let me in when I tried to visit you a couple of years ago?" I wasn't expecting any sort of apology or the start of a real relationship. I knew it was too late for that, and I was saddened by the fact that the father I was going to meet was a man on the verge of death. There were no expectations on my part. I just hoped I could learn a little more about myself, and perhaps put to rest a mystery that had been haunting me forever.

I called Mark as soon as I reached my hotel room near the airport. "I just got to town," I said. "How is Howard?"

After a cold, awful silence, Mark softly said, "Uh, Jeff . . . Daddy is gone."

"He's gone? What time did he die?"

Mark told me that Howard had passed away around 11 a.m., close to the time when I'd boarded my plane. We talked for a few more minutes, and I agreed to come visit him at Howard's apartment within the next couple of hours.

When I hung up the phone, the emotions began to hit me. Grief came first. I'd thought so much about the conversations I'd hoped to have with my father; finding him gone before I'd even arrived was the last thing I'd expected or prepared for. For a moment, I couldn't breathe; the whole world just seemed to stop. I sat there, crying.

Grief then turned to anger. Once again, a member of my family had let me down. Once again, I'd made an effort to forge a connection, and once again I'd have nothing to show for it. I found myself thinking, *That bastard couldn't wait for me! He knew I was coming—so he died just to get out of seeing me again!* For almost an hour, I paced the room, tears streaming down my face.

Eventually, I pulled myself together and drove to Howard's apartment. Mark buzzed me in. What I saw when I entered the apartment made my heart sink a bit lower. Papers and trash were strewn everywhere. The living room had three sofas, which combined would still not make one good one. A stained mattress was leaning against the wall behind one of the sofas, next to a lounge chair that looked as if it had been salvaged from a dump. The dining area had a table piled high with papers and dirty dishes. In the bedroom was a king-size bed on which mattresses of various sizes were stacked in no particular order, alongside a mirrored dresser covered with junk. The one thing that really stuck with me was a plastic baseball trophy. I picked it up and saw that my brother Robert had received it when his Little League team won the district championship. I hadn't even known that Robert played baseball.

I felt nauseated by what I saw. As I glanced around the apartment, wondering how anyone could live this way, I thought for a moment that I'd never seen anything like it in my life. But then I remembered that wasn't quite true. My mother's bedroom back in Cape was almost as bad—and the basement of her house, filled with a lifetime's worth of discarded junk, was even worse. I suppose Miss Helen had always recoiled from the idea of cleaning house because her own mother had spent a lifetime doing that for white folks.

I found myself on one of the living room sofas, leafing through the documents and photos in a box that was sitting there. There were snapshots of a young Howard in an army dress uniform, posing at Fort Leonard Wood in Missouri. I'd never heard that my father had been in the military. I came across his high school diploma from the black school in Cape Girardeau. I'd always thought he'd grown up in Arkansas. I was surprised to discover a marriage certificate that showed that he and my mother had been married in Mississippi in 1956. Little by little, a sketch of the man I'd never known anything about began to emerge.

The last item in the box was a notebook in which Howard seemed to have jotted down his last wishes. I glanced at it, unwilling to think very much about the reality of his death. I remember reading one sentence aloud to Mark, in which Howard expressed his hope that he would be remembered as a "good father and a caring and tenatious [sic] person." Mark laughed long and hard at that. Howard's notebooks ended with a list of his children. My heart sank a bit when I saw that mine was the only name he misspelled.

Mark then took me to meet a neighbor and friend of Howard's. "Alvin" was a bit heavyset, tall with a warm face and a dark complexion. He seemed a nice enough fellow.

"You're the lawyer, right?" he asked me. "Howard always talked about his son the lawyer. This is your first time here?"

"No, I tried to visit him a couple years ago, but I couldn't get in."

"Now, wait a minute," Alvin said. "Howard told us that you were supposed to come visit, but that you never came."

Mark immediately jumped in. "Alvin, you know how much of a liar Howard was. He didn't answer when Jeff here rang his bell because he didn't want his son to see how he was living. You know what he was like, Alvin. Tell his son how mean and hateful that niggah was."

Alvin obliged. He told me that Howard would deliberately clog his sink so that the other apartments would develop plumbing problems, then go to management and blame it on everyone else. One time, Howard sent Alvin a forged letter that was supposed to be from Alvin's girlfriend, telling him that she was in love with someone else and that she wanted to break up. Howard had evidently had a spat with Alvin and was attempting revenge. Later, I spoke with some of the other people in the building. They all had horror stories about this man who was my father.

After a few hours, I returned to my hotel room with a deep sense of emptiness in my heart. As the night wore on, I found I couldn't stay there—the walls just felt too close—so I decided to take a walk. The area around the airport in Los Angeles was quite barren and lifeless that night, with few cars and even fewer pedestrians. I wished I had someone to talk to, to share what I'd been experiencing, perhaps to hold me close. But on that chilly Los Angeles night, I was alone. All I could feel was sadness—sadness for the life this man had led, sadness that I'd never gotten the chance to meet him, but most of all, sadness for what I wasn't feeling. I wasn't experiencing the emotions a person should feel at the loss of a parent.

The next day, there was a family gathering at the home of Howard's stepsister, Geneva. I'd first learned about her from Howard's doctor, who had mentioned that he'd spoken to my aunt. Later, I'd called her, saying, "You will have to forgive me, but I don't really know or remember you."

With a soft chuckle, she said, "Oh, don't worry about that, baby. You were too young." Geneva had actually taken Howard to the hospital and had visited him there every day. I was looking forward to meeting Geneva. She seemed to be a genuinely sincere person.

Sunday was a bright sunny day with a definite chill in the air. Geneva lived in a very nice house on a wide street. When I arrived, I found myself in a room full of strangers—all relatives I'd never heard of or met. The only person I recognized was my brother Mark. But I was the new thing everyone wanted to see—after all, they'd all heard about "Howard's youngest" but had never met me. I spent the afternoon and evening saying polite hellos to one person after another, shaking the hands of people I'd never seen before, and repeating names I'd never heard and that I would forget within a few moments.

These strange circumstances made me feel uncomfortable, and worse was the fact that no one seemed to have any pleasant memories of Howard to share—not at all what one would expect at a family gathering after a death. Geneva talked to me a little about Howard's ordeal in the hospital, and about how he'd deteriorated from a man of over three hundred pounds to a wasted shadow just half that size.

"Did Howard ever talk about me?" I asked.

"Yes, he did," Geneva replied. "He talked all the time about his youngest son and how proud he was of him." But Geneva could think of no specific details that Howard had ever mentioned, and I could think of nothing more to ask.

As for Mark, when I tried to get him to tell me more about my father, he simply said, "That niggah gonna rot in hell! He was mean and evil, Jeff, and you should be glad you didn't meet him." When I glanced at the others gathered in the room, their faces wore looks of agreement.

I did my best to paste a smile on my face and hide my anguish. I would have liked to get to know these people, many of whom seemed kind and friendly, but the shadow of my father loomed over the occasion. I made my excuses as soon as I could. "I think I'm going to have to get going. I have a very early flight tomorrow." Mark needed a ride back to Howard's apartment, so he joined me.

In the car, I finally let it out. "Man, this has been very difficult for me. I came out here to see my father, and he died before I got the chance. And now I meet all these nice people whom I never knew about. None of this makes any sense. I feel bad for leaving, but it's hard for me to meet them like this."

In a comforting tone that I had never heard before from any of my brothers, Mark said, "I know, Jeff. I told the family that this has been really hard on you, but they just wanted to meet you. They always heard about 'the baby,' but they'd never seen you. So, I can understand where you're coming from, and I think they do too."

Mark then told me about his last moments with Howard. "Jeff, this has been hard on me too. When I saw him, I barely recognized him. I could tell that it was only going to be a matter of time. It was bad, Jeff—really bad. When I carried him down the stairs to take him to the VA hospital, he knew he wasn't going home again."

Mark went on, "Howard kept asking me, 'Do you really think Jeff's coming?' He didn't want you to see how he was living and the type of person he was. That's why he didn't let you in a couple years ago. What was sad for me was the way he was going out. I told him, 'Look around you. Look at the life you've led. Now you're paying for it.' You die the way you live, Jeff, and he died in a miserable way."

Now Mark had tears in his eyes. "Jeff, no one came to visit him, not even the pastor from his church. It made me realize that I don't want to go out that way. I'm going to be in touch with my kids. I'm going to be a better father and a better person than he was. And you and me need to come together more as brothers, too. They be cracking on you at home, saying this and that about you, but I tell them, 'Jeff did his thing. He stayed in school and got out.' I tell them that you're my hero. You didn't fall into that stuff we all did."

I had never heard such emotion from Mark before. We arrived at the apartment, hugged, and said goodbye.

My return trip to DC was a blur. I tried to focus on the good things: meeting new family, getting closer to my brother Mark, and finally closing a chapter in my life. But I felt empty and sad. More than Howard had died on that trip.

Once I got home, there was a phone call I had to make. I was grateful when she finally picked up.

"Mother, why didn't you tell me about him?" I asked. "You said he treated you bad. But you never told me anything like what I heard while I was out in LA."

There was a pause and a deep breath before my mother spoke. "I guess I just didn't want to think about those times any longer. I just wanted to get it all behind me."

I fell silent, not knowing what to say or ask.

We talked for a little while longer. I was a bit surprised to hear how solemn my mother seemed at Howard's passing. If anyone had the right to be angry at him and to celebrate his death, it would be her. Yet there was no hatred or bitterness in her voice as we talked about him. Maybe there was a happy memory or two that helped her forgive him and perhaps even feel some sadness at his death—I didn't ask and I don't know.

When I hung up, I felt as though my relationship with my mother had changed somehow. I couldn't forget anything about our past—the turmoil we'd lived through and the endless disappointments I'd suffered. But now I felt I was ready to try to understand her, not as my mother, but simply as a person.

><

How DO YOU tell your mother you've been lying to her for almost ten years?

It took about thirty years to finally want to have an adult conversation with my mother. I hadn't seen her or my hometown for a long time, and returning this time, I felt ashamed, a failure. Everything about Cape was foreign to me. I didn't know the place anymore, and my childhood home had long been lost.

It took a while for me to find the latest place Miss Helen had moved to. My heart sank a bit as I drove through the dilapidated neighborhood that she was now calling home. Much like when I made my way through some of the desperate places in Africa, one thought came to my mind: *This is not my home.*

Typically, the front door to her house was unlocked, so I walked right in. She was sitting enjoying some television program, as she normally did on a weekend morning, and I was surprised that she was home alone. This visit was like my other visits: unannounced. There never seemed to be any quiet time when I was growing up, and coming without telling her usually ensured at least a little bit of time alone together.

Although I was good at making silent entrances, I didn't want to startle her. "Hope you're watching something good," I announced.

She looked up to see who it was and said, "Well, I had a feeling you were going to show up." I enjoyed seeing the slight look of surprise on her face. She arose and darted over to give me a warm greeting. I always looked forward to hugging my mother. As a kid, there never seemed to be enough of such motherly affection.

We did our catching up and then I got to it. "Mother, there are some things I want to talk to you about." I had been thinking of what to say, trying to explain why I had returned home when I had professed the desire to never do such a thing. She made herself some tea as I went to the living room to have the chat. Before she came in, I gazed over the items that adorned the space. She still had some awful multicolored clay creations of mine prominently displayed alongside whatever awards I earned in high school and college. There were also the many pictures of me and my brothers. I could barely recognize myself as the nappy-headed little kid in the school pictures. I always thought it strange how fondly I looked back on those times.

I was a bit nervous as she came into the room. She sat next to me on the couch and I took a deep breath as I began. "Mother, I know I've told you and you've thought that I've been working for ███████████ ███ in all the years since I moved out to DC back in '93. But, the truth is . . . " I couldn't help but pause. After looking down for a moment or two, I said, "During this whole time, I've been working for the CIA."

I looked at her intently to see what sort of reaction she was going to have. She just sat there, slightly nodding her head. She looked at me and said nothing.

I continued telling her the type of life I had been living over the years. All the while, I had difficulty looking directly at her as I spoke. I then said, "I've had a lot of trouble with them and they fired me. I'm suing them for discrimination, and I wanted to tell you because I can't lie to you anymore."

She looked at me with a mother's conviction and said, "If you feel they treated you wrong, then you should fight it. I know you wouldn't say that unless it was the truth. So, I don't blame you for standing up for yourself."

I was so comforted by what she had to say. I didn't know whether she believed me or not about the CIA, but I was glad and somewhat surprised at the confidence she expressed in me.

I held her hands as I talked. "You know, I don't know if you knew it or not, but I had a really tough time growing up here." I surprised myself by bringing up the past and was caught off guard by my own feelings, so I actually had to fight back tears as I continued, "I didn't really feel as if I belonged or anyone wanted me around."

"Why, what was wrong?" she asked, almost challenging what I was confessing. She went on, "Well, I know you did always seem so distant. You know, just sort of by yourself a lot. And I thought lately you were having some difficulty in whatever, with the way you've been moving around so much." This was the first time I had heard her express any such concern. She knew me better than I thought.

"It's really hard for me to figure out why I was so different from everyone. I mean, I was the only one of the brothers to go to college and I didn't fall into the same issues like everyone else seemed to." With that last statement I had to pause slightly, as only afterward did I realize the pain it might have caused her. I continued, "What made me so different? I mean, even those who came after me, like some of my nieces and nephews, fell into the same troubles."

She was gazing at me with those deep brown eyes that always seemed so serious. "Well, you just didn't want those things."

I then said, half-jokingly, "You know what? It sort of makes me think that maybe, just maybe, I'm not your son. Look at the evidence: I was born in a different hospital, I went to college, and all the other differences."

She was always good at throwing my jokes back in my face. "Heh. Well, where do you think you came from?" She jovially turned her head away from me and gave me the hand. "Maybe they did switch babies on me."

"Well, I really don't look like any of you." I said, still laughing. I couldn't understand why I was suddenly so relaxed after so much strife.

"You look just like your father, that should be proof enough for you," she said in a lighthearted but direct tone. She always became more jaded in her speech when mentioning anything about my father.

"I never had a chance to know that. I never met the man. You know what happened when I tried . . . " I broke off and dropped my head. The memory of his death still burned.

"Well, maybe you didn't need to meet him," she said with a quiet conviction.

We talked for a while longer, and it was a good start to what turned out to be one of the most enjoyable times I had as an adult with my mother. I felt good about finally telling her the truth about my professional life. I'd never intended to tell her or anyone else, but my situation had changed all that. More important, I felt that maybe I was ready to move on from the loneliness and heartache of my boyhood, just as my mother had moved on from the nightmare that was my father.

Miss Helen, her home, her family, her friends, and the black community in Cape—maybe these were all now merely the place I'd come from. They were not something I needed to belong to. They were not who I was. But neither were they something I needed to fear, to reject, and to flee.

Who was I, then? That question was still unanswered. But now, at least, I understood clearly that the answer was mine to discover, and mine alone.

# CHAPTER TWELVE

# Seeking the Undiscovered Country

D URING 2001, WHILE MY FATHER'S DEATH WAS MOVING ME TO rethink my relationship with my family and my upbringing, I was also coming to grips with the reality that the CIA was slowly but inexorably cutting me loose. The Agency had been so much more than an employer to me. It had been the cause to which I'd chosen to devote myself and a core symbol of the America I loved and wanted to serve. That's why it had been so traumatic for me when, in May 2001, an Agency panel had chosen to terminate my position as a case officer and informed me that my first level of appeal had also been rejected. Eventually, I had decided to stand up and push back, hard, by filing a lawsuit against the Agency, despite the fact that I'd been unable to find a lawyer willing to represent me.

Then, for me—and for the world—everything changed on an unusually bright and sunny September morning.

Like millions of people, I spent September 11 staring at my television, watching in horror as surreal imagery out of a disaster movie unfolded—except that it was all impossibly real. For me in Washington, the sense of shock, rage, and helplessness had its own personal tinge. When the twin towers of the World Trade Center came crashing down, I was watching a place where I had spent countless enjoyable moments—unwinding, people watching, reveling in the diversity and freedom of New York—being turned into a mountain of flaming rubble. When 7 World Trade Center later crumbled, I remembered picking up lunches from my favorite cafeteria inside that building. I knew that some of the people who'd sat near me in that courtyard enjoying their sandwiches and sodas on pleasant city afternoons were likely among the three thousand who'd perished inside those ruins.

What's more, as the horror unfolded, I knew I was watching the results of a massive intelligence failure—and not just as an ordinary citizen, but as a CIA officer who understood how it had happened and what it really meant. I had firsthand knowledge of how lax the CIA was in its role as the front line of defense against terrorists. I'd seen how case officers were incentivized not to root out terror plots but rather to make connections on the diplomatic circuit, despite the fact that very few of America's deadliest enemies hang out there. There was no Cold War, with its clear enemies and rules, and the United States was slow to make the adjustment. Worst of all, the horror was happening in New York City, the very place I'd been kicked out of by the Agency that had failed on such an unfathomable scale. The words *I should have been there, I should have been there* echoed in my head all day.

My grief and disgust only grew during the following days. I heard CIA officials publicly blaming their inability to penetrate and thwart terrorist groups on all kinds of outside forces: lack of resources, legal restrictions, excessive concern for human rights. The public relations campaign mounted by the Agency to cover its ass was incredible—and shameless. In November 2001, when Johnny Micheal "Mike" Spann, a paramilitary operations officer in the CIA's special activities division, became the first American soldier killed in combat during the invasion of Afghanistan, the Agency abandoned its usual penchant for secrecy by massively publicizing his death. The mainstream media happily played along. It seemed that no one dared mention the phrase "intelligence failure" for fear of seeming un-American.

In the same month, John Walker Lindh was captured in Afghanistan. A US citizen, raised in Maryland and California before becoming radicalized, he'd gone to Yemen to study Arabic in 1998 then traveled to Afghanistan to fight for the Taliban and offer support to Osama bin Laden and al-Qaeda. The very existence of Lindh represented a truth that the Agency didn't want to face: if a skinny white kid from the Bay Area could knock on the door of the Taliban and be welcomed in, then claims that the Agency didn't have the personnel to penetrate such groups were necessarily false.

Of course, I had personal reasons for being particularly angry about the Agency's PR campaign. I couldn't help wondering what I could have contributed to America's counterintelligence efforts as a skilled, well-trained field officer with a nontraditional background—a black man able to speak Farsi—if I'd only been given the resources and the support I needed. I'm not claiming I could have prevented the 9/11 attacks. But there's no way to know what someone like me might have accomplished, especially as part of a team of similarly well-trained, well-supported officers.

Call me naive, but in the months after 9/11, I was wondering whether I might get a call from the Agency, despite the conflict that had arisen between us. My hopes were raised when I heard that the government was inviting job applications from individuals with knowledge of the Middle East and language abilities in Farsi and Arabic. Mulling the situation, I decided that, if the Agency did call and ask me to return to duty, I would be big about it. I would put our differences aside, drop my lawsuit, and willingly offer my services to my country—just as I'd always dreamed of doing.

I never did get that call inviting me to return to duty. Instead, I was asked to visit Agency headquarters one final time—not to receive a new assignment in the war against terror, but to receive final, formal notification that my last appeal had been denied and that my connection with the Agency was no more.

The date was October 1, 2001, less than a month after September 11, and John Brennan, the Agency's newly appointed deputy executive director, was charged with delivering the bad news. I had met with Brennan once before when he was George Tenet's chief of staff. Tenet had always professed a willingness to meet with any employee who had concerns about the organization, so after filing my EEOC complaint, I attempted to take him up on his offer. Instead, I was given an audience with Brennan. During that meeting, Brennan had told me that, as far as he knew, there had been no cases of racial discrimination within the Agency.

Today, his job was to indirectly reiterate his judgment that the Agency had never treated its minority employees unfairly. Brennan barely looked me in the eye as he spoke.

"Jeff, I wanted to come down and personally let you know that the director has turned down your appeal. As of this meeting, your employment with the Agency has been terminated." He looked at me and paused, as if expecting a reaction. I sat back in my chair and said nothing. Brennan then added, "However, in order to allow you to make a smooth transition from the Agency to whatever direction you wish to take, you will remain on the payroll for an additional six months." Again, I said nothing. I had nothing to say to him. After a moment, he rose and left.

I thought it was a little odd that the deputy executive director of the CIA would take the time to come down to an outbuilding for a two-minute meeting informing an employee that he was being fired, especially so soon after 9/11, when you might assume that he was pretty busy. The administrative officer handling my final paperwork commented on it too. "And it's the first time I've seen them give six months' extra pay," she remarked. "Three months is usually the most. I guess they want you to see that they have given careful consideration to your situation and that there are no hard feelings."

My response was just a nod and a simple "uh-huh." Somehow, I didn't share her optimistic view of the situation. I signed the paperwork and departed. My link to the CIA was finally severed once and for all.

Soon thereafter, through a friend of a friend, I finally found an attorney who was willing to take on the CIA. I was quite surprised when I first met Mark Zaid. He'd already established himself as an authority in legal battles related to national security issues, but he was very youthful looking; as I later learned, he was actually a few months younger than me. We talked over my case, and I explained that I'd filed my own suit against the Agency.

Zaid was frank in discussing the obstacles I'd be facing. "Of course," he said, "you do know that not only is your career in the CIA over, but I doubt you'd have any opportunity to work in the intelligence community in general."

"Yeah, that has been obvious for quite some time," I said. If anything, the 9/11 attacks had made my situation worse. The fact that I'd been fired by the CIA at a time when the country was shoring up its resources to fight a war on terrorism made it obvious that I was considered tainted—a marker few potential employers would be inclined to ignore.

He continued, "And you do realize that, given the women's class action from a few years ago and their hesitancy to give in again, they may come after you pretty hard. After all, you're the first black officer to ever file suit against the CIA."

The words hit me like a tornado. "Are you kidding? I'm the first?"

"There have been others who have made complaints," he said. "But as far as I know, you're the first to actually file in court."

It took me a moment to absorb this startling fact. "Well," I said, "someone has to be first, and it might as well be me."

Zaid agreed to take my case, and we shook hands on our new partnership. I was happy to know that there was finally someone fighting on my side. Before leaving his office, I offered a final observation. "This is sure to launch some conspiracy theories around Langley—a black employee hiring a Jewish lawyer to sue the Agency." Knowing the political attitudes of the Reagan disciples who staffed the Agency, I was only half joking.

Several weeks later, I got the first inkling as to the Agency's reaction to my lawsuit. Although I was no longer a CIA employee, I was still required to call in periodically during the initial months, when I was technically on payroll. The calls were normally very brief pro forma exchanges. However, during one of my call-ins, I was told that someone wanted to speak with me. It was a woman from the administrative leave office, and she sounded quite excited as she spoke.

"Jeff, did you file a lawsuit against the Agency in New York?" she asked.

I knew Zaid had served notice with the Agency that a complaint had been filed and that he had been retained as my counsel. "Yes, I did," I said.

"Well, you do realize that, even though your employment has been terminated, you're still obligated to get Agency approval for things you publicize outside of the Agency, right? The Office of General Counsel is all up in arms about what you did."

After a brief pause, I replied, "Well, what are they going to do, fire me?"

I'd fired the first shot, and I had no intention of stopping there.

Her reference to my "publicizing" my troubles at the Agency was quite accurate. In fact, I'd made it known months earlier that I had no intention of allowing the Agency to hide what was going on with me and other black employees.

In early 2001, just prior to being placed on administrative leave, I'd met with Russell Campbell in his office. He was churning out the usual canned story about how everyone at the Agency was interested in making me happy when I cut him short.

"Mr. Campbell, you know as well as I do that my career here is over. And I want you to know that I fully intend to make this situation as public as I can. I will not disclose anything about my work in the Agency that is classified, but I think the American public has a right to know how its CIA treats minorities."

Campbell said, "Well, you know, you might open yourself up to criminal proceedings if you do that."

"I'm not concerned about what they will do to me. They've already destroyed my career and thrown away everything I tried to work for." I drew nearer to him to make my last point. "I'm going to continue this fight."

It was a few months later, during the summer of 2001, that I first met with James Risen, a reporter for the *New York Times*. Risen's story about me finally appeared in the paper on March 2, 2002—delayed by several months largely because of the intense public focus on terrorism in the wake of the 9/11 attacks. The headline read, "Fired by C.I.A., He Says Agency Practiced Bias," and it recounted my efforts to build a career as a case officer, as well as the obstacles I'd encountered, which, it seemed, could only be explained by the color of my skin.

In support of my allegations, the article quoted a former case officer named Robert Baer, who'd just published his first book, *See No Evil*, based on his experiences with the Agency. Baer called the two-month, three-recruit demand I'd been given "an outrageous requirement," adding, "It often occurs that people go a whole tour of two or three years who don't recruit a single agent." Of course, Risen also offered comments from Russell Campbell and John Brennan dismissing my complaints as unfounded.

I appreciated Risen's effort to bring my story to the world, and I was glad when the article was picked up by United Press International (UPI) for wider distribution the next day. It was nice to feel that someone understood and sympathized with my plight, and for a time I even considered Risen a friend.

I received several phone calls from friends who'd had no idea about my situation, encouraging me to do what I felt was right. But others adopted a different attitude. Some friends seemed to want to distance themselves from me. Others advised that I was being headstrong and foolish: "You have to choose your battles," one of them said. Another reported hearing a colleague remark, "What is he, nuts? Taking on the CIA?" The press coverage made me fair game for everyone.

My first court appearance in connection with my lawsuit against the Agency was scheduled for mid-March 2002. I wasn't required to be present, but I wanted to be there—in part because I hadn't had occasion to visit New York City since 9/11.

I felt tense as the train departed Newark on its way to New York. I'd always enjoyed the view as the train approached the city, with the majestic Twin Towers looming as beacons of welcome. Now, however, there was just an unmistakable gap in the skyline. There was a glum silence in the train as the other passengers joined me in taking in the transformed scene.

After the brief court session, I made a point of visiting Ground Zero, the epicenter of the terrorist attack. The neighborhood was crowded with people, as I'd always known it, but the facial expressions I observed were tense and guarded, reflecting a new sense of wariness and anxiety. I remembered the areas I'd once been familiar with: the bustling courtyard between the two towers, the fountain with its odd modernist sculpture, the glass walkway that led to 7 World Trade Center, the red-and-green neon Hot Donuts Now sign at the Krispy Kreme, the express elevator leading up to the observation deck in 2 World Trade Center, the ever-busy Borders bookstore. All were now gone.

I stepped into the Stage Door Deli for a cup of coffee. I had been in that deli dozens of times, and I was delighted to see that it had not been damaged. As I sat with my coffee and gazed through the window at the people passing by, I grew angry at the reality of what I had just seen—a stark reminder of the incredible intelligence failure that had allowed 9/11 to happen. The danger was always there in plain sight, but the US intelligence machine didn't know how to look for it. I'd seen and experienced how a risk-averse CIA had turned a blind eye to real-world dangers, and how the Agency had been rendered ineffectual due to its inability or refusal to adapt to a changing world. If I'd ever had doubts about the purpose of my lawsuit, they vanished that day.

Within a few weeks, the CIA moved to have my lawsuit dismissed, invoking the rarely used "state secrets" privilege to have my case thrown out. Under this doctrine, the government can refuse to disclose information if it is determined that such disclosure would compromise national security. I found the argument somewhat laughable. Apparently I became a vital cog in America's national security machine once I filed suit, yet there'd been no such concerns when I was fired. The CIA had removed my cover retroactive to my entrance on duty, which meant the entire world was put on notice that I'd worked for them. Thus, it was all right to disclose my connection to the Agency when it suited their needs, but when my rights as a citizen were involved, absolute secrecy was demanded.

How ironic that the Agency was so afraid of the truth, when the CIA lobby is adorned with a verse from the Gospel of John: "And ye shall know the truth, and the truth shall make you free."

My own effort to let the world know the truth as I saw it led me to a CNN studio in New York on July 2, 2002. As I sat in the wings waiting to be interviewed by Connie Chung, I was feeling a little anxious. I was about to go live to share my story with thousands of people, citizens of the white America and the black America that I was widely seen as having defied, rejected, or betrayed. Would anyone care about what I had to say? Would my message really be heard?

I was summoned to the set and took my seat across from Connie, her friendly smile calming my butterflies just a bit. I was confused when a production assistant, his hands filled with an array of wires, reached around me to place a tiny speaker in my ear.

"What's that for?" I asked

"This is so you can listen to the intro."

"I don't want to hear that." I said. Though I was curious to know how it would be presented, I was somewhat reluctant to actually hear it being told by some unknown voice.

"Don't you want to hear the intro?" Connie interjected. "I think you'll like it."

"Well, okay. Let's go for it." Who was I to say no to her?

The mic was placed in my ear, and the show started. It was quite a sensation, listening to a media voice summarize my story. As I listened to the introduction, it gradually dawned on me: "I am that guy, and this is my life story." I felt as if my questions were finally being asked, my concerns were finally being addressed, my fear and anger and uncertainty were finally being shared with the world. Maybe someone would care after all.

The interview went well, and I found myself experiencing a high like no other—partly the effect of being on live television, but even more a result of the excitement I was feeling about myself. I'd been on a hell of a journey through the best and worst of black and white America, and I was still standing, still being myself, still doing what I felt was right for me and for my country.

In March 2003, the United States invaded Saddam Hussein's Iraq. This was the culmination of a months-long campaign by the administration of President George W. Bush to persuade Americans and US allies across the globe that Hussein's government represented an existential threat to the peace and safety of the world. The atmosphere of fear and anger generated by the 9/11 attacks played a major role. Although there was no evidence of involvement by Iraq in those attacks, millions of Americans mistakenly believed that Hussein had been behind the terrorist plot, and the Bush team did little to dissuade them.

Many informed observers, especially intelligence and national security experts, were outraged over the Bush administration's misuse and distortion of intelligence for political purposes. From my unique vantage point, I shared that sense of outrage. I was all too familiar with the way political and social attitudes were allowed to shape the policies and practices of the Agency, often to the detriment of America's real interests.

It was against this backdrop that I made the decision to reveal what I knew about another misguided and dangerous plot regarding Middle Eastern intelligence—not by going public, but by sharing my information with the most relevant and responsible authorities I could find.

It took a lot of effort, but with the assistance of my attorney Mark Zaid, I was able to get an audience with the Senate Intelligence Committee. Throughout my career at the Agency, I'd frequently heard about the House and Senate Intelligence Committees. These were supposed to provide secure and acceptable avenues for raising any concerns about the CIA. I'd already approached the House committee, but that had been in relation to my discrimination complaint. Now I wanted to speak with the Senate committee about my worries regarding Operation Merlin.

The meeting took place at the Senate on a sunny day in 2003. I met with two staffers, Donald Stone and Vicki Divoll. Zaid had to leave as soon as the introductions were made, because he did not have clearance to hear what I was going to talk about. As the three of us sat down in Stone's office, I made my intentions clear. "I am not here to discuss my discrimination suit with you," I said.

"That's good," Stone said, "because we're not in a position to hear anything about any ongoing litigation."

"I'm here about another matter, a CIA operation that I'm afraid may be making it easier for Iran to obtain nuclear weapons."

That got their attention.

I went on to outline the details of Operation Merlin. I explained the nature of the scheme and the way the Agency had sought to use partial, flawed designs for a nuclear device as bait in gathering accurate inside information about the Iranian weapons program. I also described what had happened in the California meeting—how Merlin himself had quickly spotted the flaw in the designs, which suggested to me that the Iranian scientists would be able to detect it as well. If that happened, our plot could backfire. Realizing that they'd been fed false data by a foreign agent, the Iranians could work their own deception on us, using Merlin as a conduit to deliver misinformation to the United States. What's more, it's possible that the Iranian scientists could actually be helped in designing a nuclear weapon by seeing fake sketches of a weapon that wouldn't work. Studying our fake designs would show them what not to do in their own program. This could enhance their ability to build a nuclear weapon, posing a potentially grave threat to world peace.

As I spoke, Divoll was dutifully taking notes. The only time she spoke was when I mentioned "the fireset," a specific component of the Merlin nuclear weapon plans. "What is that? Is that something important?" she asked.

Stone answered for me. "Yes, that's pretty important."

As the meeting drew to a close, Stone told me that they would convey my concerns to the committee members and let me know if any of them would like to speak with me.

Leaving the Senate that day, I felt a sort of satisfaction. Unfortunately, I never heard from anyone at the Senate Intelligence Committee. Years later, I would learn in a courtroom that no official document of any type regarding my interview with the Senate staffers had been submitted by Stone until well after the office had been contacted regarding the Merlin news leak—the leak that would ultimately lead to the espionage charges against me.

I'd taken the step of approaching the Senate Intelligence Committee for the same reason I'd originally applied to work at the CIA all those years before: a sincere concern for the safety and freedom of my country and a desire to serve it. Yet I was painfully aware that this dedication raised a personal question that was not easy for me to answer: What exactly is my country? Is it the black America that surrounded me when I was growing up in Cape, filled with people who rejected and belittled me because I refused to share what I saw as their acceptance of the limitations placed on their aspirations by a racist society? Or is it the white America I encountered at the Agency, largely populated by Reagan disciples who judged and pigeonholed me—perhaps deliberately, perhaps unwittingly and unthinkingly—based not on my real abilities and motives but on stupid and inaccurate racial stereotypes?

Both black and white America had places for me. But I'd always believed in and aspired to a place much bigger and much better than the ones set aside for me based on the color of my skin. I believed in an America that was greater than either the black America or the white America I knew. This was my undiscovered country, and I still longed to find it.

# PART THREE

# BLOWBACK

# CHAPTER THIRTEEN

# Desperate Times

As had been the case ever since I was fired, the days in 2003 just seemed to blend into one another. Every day involved the same handful of activities: job hunting via the Internet; networking with contacts I'd made in legal circles in Virginia, Maryland, DC, and New York; writing and rewriting the memoir I'd talked myself into tackling; and anything else I could think of to do in an effort to remain positive. Those nameless days always ended up in the same place they began. My progress might have been scant, but I nevertheless held on to hope.

In looking for work, I attempted to connect with one of the many government contractors in the DC area. I thought the fact that I'd had a prior security clearance at a respectable level might catch an employer's eye, but months passed without success. I did everything I could to build on my contacts in the legal world. I met with people and firms, attended local bar functions, and made cold calls requesting interviews with companies from DC to New York. Nothing came of my efforts. It seemed my troubled experience in the world of intelligence was casting a long shadow.

There were moments when I thought my luck was about to turn. I would hear about an open position at a government contractor like Science Applications International Corporation (SAIC), a big technology company with several locations in the DC area. The job description would tell me that I was well qualified, maybe even over-qualified. I'd get a foot in the door, participate in a couple of favorable interviews, and develop a really good vibe. Then, just when I thought a job offer was about to be made, the phone would stop ringing, the emails would stop coming, and the people I'd met and seemingly impressed would suddenly behave as if they couldn't recall meeting me.

The pattern was unmistakable, and one potential employer confirmed what I suspected: that when they'd called the Agency to check my references and confirm my security clearance, I'd been black-balled. I was devastated, hurt, and angry. But I had no choice but to keep trying—and so I did, week after dreary week.

Loneliness was another problem. My closest companions were my beloved cats, Pee Wee and Marble. They'd been with me for years, and I couldn't imagine life without them. But human relationships were another matter. I did what I could to maintain contact with friends, but I was forbidden to connect with people I knew at the Agency. In any case, I wouldn't have contacted them, not wanting to put them in an uncomfortable position. So I had to make new friends, which I found surprisingly hard, having been thrust back into the real world after years as a clandestine operative.

Determined not to be a hermit, I made it a point to get out of my apartment at least once a day. I worked out at the gym and became a regular at the local Starbucks, where I would nurse a coffee and scratch away at my book manuscript and other writing projects. But it was tough to turn the superficial acquaintances I made into any real relationships. Here I was, in my early thirties, with no job, a dwindling bank account, and almost nothing to show for the years and money I'd spent on college and law school in pursuit of the American dream. I wasn't much of a catch and I knew it.

I was sinking fast mentally. The weeks, then months, of constant effort with no results took a steady toll on my psychological strength. One day in 2003, there came a time when it seemed to me that the only solution was to put an end to my life.

I spent the better part of that lovely summer day playing with the kitties and giving them as much love as I could. As the beautiful day turned to night, I decided to get dinner from the Chinese takeout spot near my apartment. I didn't want to mess up the kitchen with cooking—it was spotless, the way I wanted it to be.

I savored every bite of the meal. The cats had been fed and were going through their after-dinner ritual of cleaning themselves and preparing for an early evening nap. I rose from my dining spot on the floor and tossed the takeout containers neatly away. It was time to act. I headed to the bathroom where, over my months of battling depression, I'd collected a trove of prescription medicines: antidepressants, sleep aids, and pain killers—from Zoloft and Paxil to an array of 'prams, benzos, and 'dones. I set them all down on the edge of the basin. *This should do it*, I thought, and I set about methodically swallowing every pill.

When I was done, I felt the need for a drink. I remembered that I'd had a half bottle of bourbon sitting on a shelf in the apartment for quite a while. *That'll make a good night cap*, I thought. It went down fast and smooth.

My throat burning from the whiskey and the pills I'd swallowed, I went to the bedroom to lie down. I felt uncommonly serene, even peaceful, for the first time in a long while. *All I have to do is go to sleep*, I thought. *It's that easy.* A welcome feeling of drowsiness soon washed over me. I could feel myself smiling. At last, something was finally going right for me.

Suddenly, I felt a sort of disturbance next to me. Was I dreaming? I forced my eyes open and saw that both Pee Wee and Marble had jumped onto the bed. That was normal behavior for them, but this time they sat staring at me for a while, with what seemed to be a sad and curious expression on their faces. Then, rather than wrestling one another for the best spot as they usually did, they both lay down next to me, purring softly. The sight was unexpectedly touching. "You don't deserve to be left alone," I whispered to them.

I reached for the phone, and after fumbling with the buttons for a few moments, I finally managed to reach one of my few speed-dial numbers—my psychiatrist's line. I greeted him, and there was a pause before he responded. I suppose he was taking in the late hour of my call and what must have been my slurred speech.

"Hello, Jeff. How are you?" His voice was professionally calm.

I can't recall exactly what I said, but I know I asked him to do me a favor: to find a good home for my beloved cats.

Now his voice had a note of urgency in it. "Why do you need me to do that, Jeff? Have you done something to yourself?"

Perturbed, I replied, "Doctor, will you please just do that for me, please?"

"I can do that, but you have to tell me why. Why do you want me to find a good home for your cats? You've been providing a good home for them, right?"

My thoughts weren't clear, and I couldn't focus on what he was saying. Finally, I responded, "I'm just worried about them, and I want to make sure they are cared for." I think the phone fell out of my hand for a minute; I know that something jarred me a little, restoring my focus. "You have to just do this for me. I don't want anything else from you, okay?"

"I'm afraid I can't do that, Jeff. I've already notified the authorities. Please let them in when they get there, and—" Either I hung up or the phone fell out of my hand again, but the call was over.

I don't remember much of what happened after that. When I try to reconstruct it, I have flashes of scenes running through my head. I remember being led out of my apartment and then waking up in a hospital. The flashbacks become more disturbing as I feel myself being strapped down to a hospital bed; I seem to remember reaching for a police officer's gun, which is what forced the hospital attendants to secure me. I feel the pain of a tube being forced down my throat and a sucking sensation in my stomach. I see bright lights and hear voices above me, speaking to me but not making any sense. I remember fighting, but I don't know whom or what I was fighting, or why.

I remember waking up in the hospital the next day, not knowing how I'd gotten there or what day it was. Because of my previous heart condition, I'd been put in the cardiac unit, the youngest of all the patients in the ward. The doctors and nurses treated me with pity and concern that I might once have appreciated, but all I could feel was a sense of disgust for myself. I refused all calls from anyone at the Agency; I didn't need or want their sympathy. The attending doctor had a heavy accent and requested that I pray with him. It was one of the first times in my life when prayer didn't seem like such a bad idea. I gave it a try, and as much as I didn't want to admit it to myself, those few moments of reflection gave me a bit of comfort.

Because I was under the care of a therapist, the hospital released me within a couple of days. I returned home to find that the door of my apartment had been badly damaged—undoubtedly by the police or the paramedics who had come to rescue me.

Otherwise, nothing in my life had changed. I still had nowhere to go, nothing to do except to keep up my painful, now public, fight against the Agency.

>‹

WITH THE HELP and support of my therapist and my friends, I began to inch back from the abyss. I renewed my personal commitment to my struggle for recognition and acceptance against the forces that were seeking to crush me.

Unfortunately, the news on that front was not good. By the spring of 2003, the Agency and the Department of Justice had already made good use of the legal strategy of venue shopping. They'd succeeded in having my case transferred from the Southern District of New York— where the discrimination I complained about actually took place—to the Eastern District of Virginia. This made sense strategically, because the Fourth US Circuit Court of Appeals is in the CIA's backyard and is known for rarely ruling against the Agency.

The government was also pressing its state secrets defense against me, saying that there was no way my claims of discrimination could even be evaluated without the presentation of classified information in open court. It's a tricky argument, one that lends itself to a catch-22. As one lawyer commented on National Public Radio while being interviewed about my case, "The theory is that the government—the executive branch—is in the best position to assess all the various factors that need to go into whether a particular item of information has national security implications or not." The result: one of the interested parties in the case is also allowed to decide what evidence may be presented.

It's hard to see how this practice can be construed as fair and unbiased. But in a country where national security interests are often presumed to trump all, the government has gotten away with it. The paranoid atmosphere of the post-9/11 period certainly did nothing to improve this imbalance.

On top of this, I soon had a new practical problem to deal with. I'd been living for months in the most frugal way I could. Piece by piece, I'd sold all of my possessions that had any value—electronic gear, items of furniture—on Craigslist. Now my savings had shrunk to the point where I could no longer afford my apartment in Virginia. I'd have to move out, and there was only one place I could go: back to where I'd started, Cape Girardeau.

I didn't relish the idea of having to return to the home where I'd never felt truly accepted, and which I'd left with such high hopes nearly two decades before. But I accepted the reality that I had no other choice. What really bothered me was the fact that I'd be forced to separate from my beloved Pee Wee and Marble. There was just no way I could bring them to live with me in Miss Helen's house. I was afraid I could never find a suitable home for these two senior felines, both of whom had now reached the ripe old age of fourteen.

I was relieved when a woman who worked at the local veterinarian's office volunteered to take them in. "Joanne" lived on a farm and had taken in several other cats over the years. I promised her that I would take them "when I got back on my feet," but Joanne simply smiled and said, "Don't worry, I'll take good care of them." Somehow I knew she was telling the truth.

I spent the next few days playing with Pee Wee and Marble, spoiling them with treats and brushings. Finally, having stuffed my remaining possessions into my car, I brought the cats in their carriers to the vet's office and dropped them off. I left a big chunk of my heart with them. And despite my sincere promises, I would never get to see Pee Wee or Marble again.

# CHAPTER FOURTEEN

# Coming Back

I MOVED BACK IN WITH MISS HELEN, WHO WELCOMED ME WITH surprising warmth and compassion. I spent a month looking for work in Cape without success. I also stayed in touch with some temp agencies in the DC area. They, too, had nothing for me. My inability to land a job wasn't just hurting me financially—it was also deepening my sense of being an utter failure.

Relief came from an unexpected source.

I decided one day to visit a classmate from Millikin who was living in suburban St. Louis, a couple of hours from Cape. "Cindy Carlson" had been a good friend during my college days, and she and her husband, "Ted," had spent years trying unsuccessfully to have a baby. I was delighted that the Carlsons had finally been able to have a daughter with the help of a friend who served as a surrogate, using Ted's sperm and an egg donated by Cindy's sister. Little "Victoria"—now three months old—was a miracle baby, and the smile she gave me when I cradled her in my big hands was a thing of beauty and joy.

I had a long, wonderful visit with Ted and Cindy, after which they invited me to stay over rather than make the two-hour drive to Cape in the middle of the night. I agreed reluctantly, not wanting to intrude on their new family, but it was an enjoyable visit for all of us.

At some point that weekend, Cindy mentioned that they were paying a babysitter to come to their home every day to watch Victoria while they both worked. Of course, I'd shared with them the problems I was having finding a job. When I heard about their childcare situation, a crazy idea popped into my head—so crazy that I couldn't believe I was even thinking it. Yet it was also the most sensible idea that had come to me in some time. After a moment's hesitation, I just went ahead and said it.

"Cindy, how about letting me stay here and watch Victoria for you? You won't have to pay me. I'll do it just for room and board. In fact, I think I'll probably have a better chance at finding work here in St. Louis than in Cape. So it could work out for you and for me too."

There I was, applying for a job as a live-in babysitter—a nanny. It's not exactly what I'd expected to be doing at age thirty-six, after earning a law degree and working as an officer for the CIA. But Cindy and Ted had no hesitation. They immediately agreed that they would be comfortable with me watching their child and living in their home. All I needed to do was get my few things from Cape, and I could start my new job as a nanny.

The next few months of my life were amazing. Unhappy as I was with my career and my legal situation, I found that spending my days caring for Victoria—returning her smiles, making her laugh, and watching her grow and learn—was a source of inexplicable pleasure.

I developed all kinds of skills I'd never been called upon to master. I became an expert at changing Victoria's diapers, soothing her when she was teething, and helping her settle in for a nap. We had fun together even when my experiments in child-rearing didn't quite work out. One day, having decided that Baby Einstein was just too weird, I came up with the idea that Victoria needed to be immersed in the world of legends and lore. I figured that a good place to start would be the story about how Pink Floyd's classic album *The Dark Side of the Moon* was produced to sync with the old movie of *The Wizard of Oz*. I propped Victoria up in her pumpkin chair and fired up the CD player. But after a few minutes of watching the film with the supposed alternative soundtrack, Victoria had switched her attention to her favorite toy, a stuffed tiger. I think she agreed with me that the old legend had been exposed as a bunch of hooey.

One thing I loved about caring for an infant was the relatively consistent schedule. Victoria had nap times interspersed among feedings, diaper changes, and time for playing. Her downtime gave me opportunities to visit every job search site I could find. I also made a habit of spending time at the library during the evenings and on weekends. I was determined to use every resource possible to search for a job, even though my efforts so far had been fruitless.

I also used my time living with Cindy, Ted, and Victoria to seek legal and political support for my case from local leaders. Back in DC, I'd already reached out unsuccessfully to people and organizations I thought would find my discrimination case to be compelling and important. I'd contacted Reverend Al Sharpton's National Action Network, Reverend Jesse Jackson's Rainbow PUSH Coalition, the American Civil Liberties Union, and other organizations. None expressed any inclination to believe me or even to hear me out.

Now I made a last-ditch effort to appeal for help. I decided to reach out to Lacy Clay, an influential politician out of St. Louis. I emailed his local office and made several calls. Much to my surprise, one call landed me a personal meeting with his staff at one of his offices on Delmar Boulevard. It was a foot in the door, at least.

It was a brisk afternoon in St. Louis as I made my way to Congressman Clay's office. I was escorted to a conference room, where I met a staff lawyer, a rather serious-looking tall man with a dark complexion and glasses, and another staff member, an older woman with grayish hair and a round, kindly face like that of Aunt Bee in the old *Andy Griffith Show*.

Introductions made, I told my whole story for what seemed like the thousandth time. I explained how I'd been discriminated against by the Agency and showed why I believed that many other black employees had received similar treatment—although I was the only one willing to take my case to court. I described my difficulties in finding an attorney to represent me and the legal strategies that the Agency and the Department of Justice were using against me. Finally, I expressed my anxieties: "I'm afraid they are going to come after me with everything they have. I can't fight this alone. I need help from someone—from Congressman Clay—from anyone."

The attorney had been taking detailed notes as I spoke. Now he dropped the pen and sat up straight in his chair. "Mr. Sterling," he said, "we will bring up your issues and concerns with the congressman." Then his tone changed. He leaned forward, looked me in the eye, shook his head slightly, and said in a quiet voice, "But I gotta tell ya, if I were in your position, man, I'd leave the country. I'd go to Canada, or wherever."

I glanced over at the other staffer. "Aunt Bee" was nodding her head in agreement.

I knew the meeting was over. I stood up and replied, "Well, that's never been an option for me. Nor should it be. Thank you for meeting with me. I do hope to hear from the congressman."

Needless to say, I never heard from Congressman Clay or anyone else from his office again. That year would have been a terrible one for me had it not been for Cindy, Ted, and Victoria.

✴

THE ARRIVAL OF 2004 gave me a new sense of promise. I made a job search decision: I would either find work near St. Louis in the next few months, or I'd return to the DC area. I had been in touch with friends in Virginia who offered me a place to stay while I looked for work. Just having a plan made me feel more purposeful and positive.

I was almost ready to give up on the St. Louis market when I decided to try taking one more shot at a job I'd seen listed online. The position was for a fraud investigator with a health insurance company called WellPoint. I didn't know much about health insurance, but I certainly knew something about conducting investigations. Within a few days of applying, I had an interview set up. That felt like a good sign, and it was. I got the job.

To say I was elated would be an understatement. I felt as if I was returning to life after a forced hiatus. This was more than just a job, this was another chance—a chance I was determined to make the most of.

The transition involved some challenges. One was the sadness I felt about losing my daily interactions with Victoria. Others were more mundane. During my period of unemployment, my bank accounts had been wiped out, and I had big debts hanging over my head: credit card balances, unpaid bills, and more. My credit rating had also been ruined thanks to a car repossession and other blows. Now I had to figure out how to get past these impediments and start over financially. I would need a place of my own to live, some new clothes fit for work, and probably a car.

Although it stung me psychologically, I realized that the only realistic option was to file for bankruptcy. At least I was able to minimize the expense by serving as my own attorney, filing pro se. Once my debts were discharged, I felt both a burden of sadness—once again, I'd experienced a failure that left me feeling ashamed and unworthy—and a sense of relief. I was once again a part of the world. I even got a cell phone.

Working at WellPoint reinvigorated my life. It turned out that being a fraud investigator for a health insurance company was a lot like being a case officer for the CIA. I did research to find targets—in this case, fraudulent patients, doctors, or pharmacies—but instead of recruiting them for information, I unearthed their wrongdoing and took steps to stop it. I eventually became very successful in Medicare fraud investigations. In 2010, I was honored by the National Health Care Anti-Fraud Association for participating in a case that received an honorable mention in the investigation-of-the-year category. I also received the 2010 Anti-Fraud Award in the investigations/criminal category from the Blue Cross Blue Shield Association.

It felt good to finally be recognized as a capable individual, able to use my knowledge and skills as an investigator without being pigeon-holed because of the color of my skin. And because Medicare fraud steals from American taxpayers and takes away money needed to provide citizens with essential health care, my work for WellPoint was another way for me to serve my country.

In addition, I found it refreshing that I no longer had to work and live under a cloud of secrecy. I had enjoyed the covertness of the CIA, but it had also made me feel cut off from ordinary life. Now I was out in the real world again, and I felt freer than I had in a very long time.

I was still waiting for a final resolution of my lawsuit against the Agency—an act of closure that I needed to lay to rest that painful episode in my life and that I still hoped would demonstrate, to myself and to the world, that I was a worthy American who'd been wrongfully deprived of the opportunity to serve my country. But even without that, I was feeling a lot better about life. Having a productive job, being able to use my intelligence and my skills in a worthwhile way, taking care of my own needs while contributing to society—all of these things made a huge positive difference in my outlook.

The biggest thing still missing was the thing I'd been lacking since the day Sandy walked out on me: someone to share my life with. I wasn't happy about being alone, and I knew I wouldn't be satisfied to go through the rest of my existence that way. I'd loved being married, and I wanted to experience again the sense of intimate sharing, unquestioned acceptance, and mutual support it had provided me.

In my quest for a new life partner, I had to go through what millions of other divorced or widowed people have gone through—the strange experience of returning to the dating scene after years away. Like millions of others, I took advantage of the new world of dating websites as a way to break the ice.

My first few digitally arranged dates didn't do much to enthrall me with excitement about dating again. There was the woman who turned out to have used a friend's picture on her profile rather than her own, the woman who refused to believe that my online photo was real (it was), and the woman who showed up for the date with a gag-gle of her male friends ("I don't go anywhere without my crew!" she cheerfully explained). I found myself thinking, *I don't remember dating being this weird.*

I finally connected with a woman who appeared to be a little less odd than the rest. Holly was a social worker living in a suburban com-munity to the west of St. Louis. Like me, she'd found online dating to be frustrating, so she insisted we have several email and phone con-versations prior to meeting—a promising start indeed. I had a good feeling about this one, and that made me all the more nervous when we arranged our first face-to-face encounter.

On July 29, 2004, I arrived early at Cicero's, a local institution in the U-City Loop. I was familiar with the area from my law school days. I settled in at a table with a good view of the front and rear en-trances, a habit I'd developed as an officer for the Agency.

By 7:30, she was a half an hour late. By 7:45, I had given up on her. I decided to just relax, have a couple of beers, and maybe shoot a game of pool. No longer on guard, I took a seat near the pool tables. For some reason, I glanced toward the back door, and that was when I saw her, walking in my direction. I knew it was her without her saying a word. Trying to play it cool, I casually placed my glass on the table as she stepped toward me and said, "Jeffrey?"

I paused for a moment, lost in how beautiful she appeared. Finally, I managed to get out a reply—"Holly?"—and we shook hands.

"I'm so sorry. I got stuck at a train crossing. And wouldn't you know it, the train was a really long one!"

The truth was that I'd already forgotten about her lateness.

Over the next few hours, we had dinner, strolled the loop, and made our way to another local hot spot called the Pin-Up Bowl to extend our conversation. All the nervousness I'd had about meeting her disappeared. As the evening wore on, I found myself smiling more than I had in years—and it felt good.

Before we knew it, the time was nearing 2 a.m. Since we both had to work the next day, we reluctantly agreed to call it a night. As I walked her to her car, the heavens opened and it began to rain heavily, so our walk turned into a sprint. We sat in the car for a while, wet, talking and laughing, neither wanting the date to end. I finally got up the courage to do what I'd wanted to do all night—to kiss her. The torrent of rain streaming down the car windows provided the perfect backdrop for a brief kiss that seemed to last forever.

We both knew there would be a second date. And that second date was all the confirmation I needed of the feelings Holly had stirred in me. We were standing on the metro platform waiting for the train after the concert we'd attended. I took Holly in my arms and, with a big smile on my face, said, "You know something, Ms. Holly?"

She looked up at me with her piercing hazel eyes. "What's that, Mr. Sterling?"

"We're going to get married someday, barefoot and on a beach."

With a twinkle in her eye, she replied, "Oh, really?"

I held her tighter, "Yep. And by an Elvis impersonator."

She burst into one of her infectious laughs. "Well, I'm okay with the beach and barefoot. I'm not so sure about the Elvis impersonator."

"No use fighting it, I've decided." We laughed together.

Things moved quickly after that. By September, I'd moved into Holly's villa in suburban O'Fallon. More important, I kept no secrets from Holly. I wanted her to know everything about who I was, who I had been, and even who I wanted to be. She didn't flinch when I told her about my tribulations with the CIA, my divorce, and even my suicide attempt, which was the episode I was most worried about sharing. Her response was simple: "I'm glad you didn't succeed."

The wonder of this woman delighted me in ways that were both unfamiliar and sorely needed. I was filled with a sense of hope and happiness that I hadn't felt for a long time. I had a new home, a new career, a new love, a new life.

# CHAPTER FIFTEEN

# America Returning to Me

In August 2005, I learned the final outcome of my discrimination case against the Agency. The previous fall, the judges of the Fourth US Circuit Court of Appeals had decided that my constitutional rights were of no concern when set against the national security of the country—at least the national security as defined by the CIA. It was a pro forma decision that aligned with many other decisions previously issued by the same court, but Judge J. Harvie Wilkinson III added a shot at the end of the unanimous ruling, as if he wanted to make sure I knew where I stood in America: "We recognize that our decision places, on behalf of the entire country, a burden on Sterling that he alone must bear . . . in order to protect a greater public value." Thus, the court made it clear that I was to suffer the indignities of racial discrimination as my contribution to the security of the nation.

Now, in 2005, the Supreme Court refused to hear my appeal. I'd done what I could for America, but the terms of our relationship were never the ones I would have chosen. All I could do now was set aside my disappointment and my hurt and try to move on with my life. But within a few months, I would discover that America was not yet done with me.

The first warning signs consisted of vague rumors. My attorney, Mark Zaid, had many connections in the worlds of intelligence and national security. When juicy stories were circulating, Zaid was likely to hear about them. In late 2005 and early 2006, he shared with me some disturbing tales he'd been hearing about the *New York Times* writer who had written about my discrimination case, James Risen. "It seems he's been writing an expose about the CIA," Zaid told me, "including some dirt on some secret Iranian project you were involved in."

"That's good," I said. "It was a big problem, and I'm glad it's going to get exposed."

"Maybe so," he said. "But some people I know at the Agency are saying they're hopping mad and they're determined to figure out who Risen's sources were. And some are saying that you've got a target on your back."

"That's crazy," I replied. "I never talked with Risen or anyone else about that project, except for the two Senate committee staffers who interviewed me."

"I understand, but I hope you can prove that. You may have to."

It didn't take long for the rumors to assume a more tangible shape.

One warm summer day in 2006, I was just returning home from work when a blue late-model car pulled into the driveway. A man and a woman emerged and approached me.

"Hello, Mr. Sterling," the woman said. "My name is Ashley K. Hunt, and this is my colleague 'Doug Savage.' We're agents with the FBI. Do you mind if we come inside and have a talk with you?"

I wasn't happy with having them show up like this, unannounced and uninvited. "You can talk to me right here," I replied.

Savage held out a copy of a hardcover book. I caught the title: *State of War.* "Have you ever seen this book?" he asked.

"Never," I replied truthfully. Hunt started to ask me another question, but I didn't let her continue. "It bothers me that you just show up like this. Have you spoken to my attorney prior to coming here?"

"No," Savage said.

"But we're concerned because of what's in this book," Hunt said. She then pulled out a picture of a nondescript man, possibly of Middle Eastern descent. "Have you seen this person around? This man is an Iranian national, and we have reason to think he may be surveilling you. If we could just have a minute to talk inside—"

"I'd know if some Iranian or anyone else was targeting me as you say. And again, you are not coming in."

They got the message. Hunt handed me a business card. "Please give us a call. Maybe we can arrange a time to talk." At the same moment, Savage handed me a piece of paper. It was a summons to appear before a grand jury in Virginia. I noticed a smirk on his face as I glanced at the document.

I made an effort to keep my voice as calm as possible. "Might I suggest you go through my attorney if you plan on any future visits? I certainly plan on speaking with him about this. Have a good day."

I turned and went inside the house. For a few minutes, my whole body was shaking so violently with anger and disgust that I was unable to call Zaid. Finally, I dialed his number and let him know what had happened.

I hadn't spoken to him in a while. He had an uncertain tone in his voice that I wasn't accustomed to. "I've heard rumblings about a grand jury," he said, "but no one's been in touch with me about it or about anything else related to you."

"What do you think I should do?"

"Well, I'm not in a position to represent you in any potential criminal matter. But I do know someone who might help."

That's how I came to know Edward MacMahon Jr., a veteran attorney with offices in Virginia and DC. Based on my own legal experience, I had a pretty clear idea of what I would want in a criminal defense attorney. The personality I'd seek would be that of an extrovert—someone who appears very confident, with what you might call a respectable air of arrogance. Ed fit the bill, and I was pleased when he agreed to become my attorney. I gave him the summons I'd received, along with Ashley Hunt's contact information, leaving the whole matter in his hands.

I was a little nervous about telling Holly about the sudden reemergence of my past. I was happily surprised that her reaction was not only understanding but also unquestioningly supportive. It confirmed that I had found someone special in her, and that this relationship was one that I was never going to give up.

Over the next few days and weeks, I learned more about what the feds were after. The book they'd shown me was James Risen's *State of War: The Secret History of the CIA and the Bush Administration*. It had been published in January 2006, and it contained a series of explosive disclosures about American intelligence. Among other allegations, the book said that the National Security Agency had been engaged in a massive domestic spying program and that US intelligence agencies were well aware that Iraq did not have weapons of mass destruction, though they hid that fact from both the general public and the president.

The significant malfeasance involved in Operation Merlin—particularly the fact that the botched operation had actually helped Iran obtain classified information about nuclear weapons designs rather than thwarted their efforts—played a relatively minor role in the book. But perhaps because it was the single most damaging accusation in the book leveled against the CIA itself, this was the part of the story that had caused the Agency and its friends in the Department of Justice to be bent on retaliation. The fact that my name and James Risen's were linked—if only through the article about me that Risen had published in the *Times*—seemed to be reason enough to put me in their crosshairs.

During this time, I was also getting calls from friends to let me know that the two FBI agents had been paying them visits. They had even dropped in on Holly's family in Illinois. I was fuming, but there was nothing I could do about it. I wondered when I would hear from Ed about my appearance before the grand jury, but word never came. Holly and I did our best to put the episode behind us and focus on our life together.

Just when I was getting to the point of feeling that the witch hunt might be over, Holly got summoned to appear before the grand jury empaneled in Alexandria, Virginia. She found the prospect terrifying. She promptly hired a lawyer to help her through the ordeal, but the weeks leading up to her appearance were nerve-racking. I wanted to be supportive, but it seemed best for me to avoid the subject altogether, since every time we discussed it she became very upset. I'd never wanted the horrors of my conflict with the Agency to impact her, but now that had become unavoidable.

When Holly was finally scheduled to make her trip to Virginia, I was out of town on business. When I returned home, I found her shaken up from the unexpected grilling she'd received at the hands of the US attorneys. I was holding her in my arms, trying to bring some comfort to her and myself, when the phone rang.

Holly picked up, and I watched her face quickly turn pale. After just a moment, she hung up and began to sob.

"What's going on?" I asked

"My lawyer is on his way here. The FBI is coming with a search warrant."

Almost immediately, there was a knock at the door. It was Savage with a search warrant and a team of federal agents filling our front yard right behind him. I had no choice but to let them in. Then I rushed to call Ed MacMahon.

"I know about the FBI," Ed said. "They just called me. Stay out of their way and let them do their thing. You might even want to leave until they're finished."

"No. I'm staying. They're not chasing me from my home." I hung up and took a seat on the sofa, trying to console Holly. As I embraced her, the agents swarmed, opening drawers, looking in cupboards, checking out the contents of closets. They quickly zeroed in on our home office, where they set about rifling through file folders.

"Why are they doing this? Why are they in our home?" Holly cried.

"It's called, 'Let's teach the nigger a lesson,'" I responded angrily. I glared at Savage as I spoke.

Holly's lawyer arrived in a few minutes. His name was "Charles Baker." (I later discovered that he and I had been law school classmates.) Charles sat on the living room sofa with us as the chaos continued.

"This whole thing is completely fucked up," I told him. "They obviously planned it based on when we would be getting home. I guess they figured they needed to get here before Holly and I could destroy stuff. Well, let them do whatever they want. There's nothing to find, and they know it."

I must have been getting a little loud, because Charles motioned for me to calm down. Leaving Holly with him, I walked out to the deck and had a seat, seething with rage.

When I returned inside a few minutes later, Savage came up to me and pointed at the computer in our office. "Is that your work computer?" he asked.

"That's right," I said.

"That's what we thought," he said, and handed me a letter.

It was from "Perry Eisen," the head of my department at Well-Point, and it said, in effect, "We've been asked by the FBI for your work computer, and we've agreed to hand it over."

Wearing his characteristic smirk, Savage signaled to one of the other agents to unplug the computer and pack it up for removal. But when he began rifling through the computer bag on the floor nearby, I stepped close to him. Savage looked at me nervously, perhaps thinking the angry black man was about to attack.

"Excuse me," I said. "The letter only mentions the computer, nothing else."

Savage reached for the letter and read it, probably for the first time. He muttered, "Okay," and dropped the bag in disgust.

When the agents left, Holly and I realized they'd only been there for about thirty minutes, though it had felt to us like an eternity. When your home is violated like that, it seems as if your life has been invaded. Knowing that our own government was behind the violation made it that much worse.

I figured I ought to call Perry Eisen at WellPoint. I took it for granted that I was no longer an employee of the company.

"Hi, Perry. I got your letter, and they've taken the computer."

"I know and I'm sorry," Perry said, sounding apologetic. Before moving to the insurance industry, he'd been a federal prosecutor, and he must have had a vivid understanding of what Holly and I had been through. I appreciated his empathy.

"I guess this means I no longer have a job," I said.

I was surprised at his answer. "Well, our viewpoint is that you're innocent until proven guilty, and that hasn't occurred. So you still have your job."

I hung up, grateful that—at least for a time—I didn't have unemployment to worry about.

I walked around the house to survey the aftermath of the intrusion. The agents had been surprisingly neat. Other than the empty spot under the desk where my computer tower had sat, there was really no sign of their having been there.

I returned to Holly, who was still visibly shaken. I held her in my arms, not knowing what to say. With eyes glassy from crying, she looked up to me. "Let's leave, go out for dinner, something. I just can't be here right now." We went out for a bite to eat, trying to either make sense of what had happened or forget about it. We failed at both.

That night, Holly and I hung onto each other as tightly as we could. It had been a terrible day, but at least it had started and ended with us together, still in love.

# CHAPTER SIXTEEN

# Goodbye to the Past

M Y LEGAL EXPERIENCE TOLD ME THAT AN INDICTMENT AND arrest usually follow closely behind the execution of a search warrant. But nothing happened. There was no further word from the FBI or anyone. Several calls to Ed all yielded the same response: "I haven't heard anything. I'm not sure what they're doing." Days turned into weeks, weeks into months. Holly and I gradually moved on with our lives together.

By the end of 2006, I was ready to ask Holly to be my wife. We didn't necessarily need to get married. Nothing the FBI, the CIA, or a grand jury could do would ever tear us apart. But I'd known for a long time that marriage was in our future, and the idea of a commitment to stay together forever was deeply appealing to me.

I wanted the proposal to be perfect, and I wanted it to be a surprise. I picked Christmas as the date to pop the question. I used my CIA skills to sneak one of her favorite rings out of the house so a jeweler could use it to measure her size, and I even wrote some silly little Christmas poems to go along with the gift. Everything seemed set until the day I went to pick up the ring. The woman at the jewelry store asked me, "Is Holly the name of the bride-to-be?"

I was shocked, because I knew I'd never mentioned her name. "How do you know that?"

"She was in here the other day, and she mentioned that you'd bought her some earrings here once before."

Now I was growing nervous, fearing that weeks of planning had just been fouled up.

The clerk continued, "She said she was trying to come up with a gift for you that would be better than the one she got you last year. I told her, 'Oh, yes, I know him. He was in here recently.'"

My jaw dropped. "You didn't tell her what I bought, did you?"

"Oh no. I didn't let on. She doesn't suspect a thing." I wasn't comforted by the clerk's accompanying laugh.

My anxiety quickly faded when I saw the beautiful ring I had picked out. Much like our life, it had twists and turns and was held together with an unseen bond. I couldn't wait until Christmas to put it on her finger.

On Christmas Day, after all our preliminary gifts were exchanged, it was time for the main event. I had recorded two Christmas poems and loaded them on the MP3 player that was one of Holly's gifts. With headphones on, she laughed as she listened to the first poem. Then, as the second poem started, I knelt before her, the ring extended toward her.

"Oh, Jeffrey!" she said, as tears welled up in her eyes. Her hand shook as I put the ring on her finger.

With a smile on my face, I asked, "Is that a yes?"

She gave me the most wonderful kiss I had ever received. "Yes, yes, I'll marry you!"

We were married in Jamaica the following June. The only issues we encountered in the weeks leading up to that wonderful trip were delays in getting our passports. I was worried that one or both of us had somehow ended up on a no-fly list, a not uncommon mishap in those post-9/11 years. But my passport finally arrived at the last minute via FedEx, while Holly was able to use her driver's license and a copy of proof that she was waiting for her passport.

We got married on the beach and barefoot, just as I'd predicted— though Holly got her way and vetoed my idea of having an Elvis impersonator serve as the officiant.

>‹

MONTHS AND YEARS passed with no further rumblings from the government. I was beginning to feel that maybe, just maybe, my nightmare conflict with the Agency was all behind us. Like millions of other Americans, Holly and I quietly celebrated in November 2008 when Barack Obama achieved what we thought we'd never see by becoming America's first black president.

Despite the joy at having a new life with Holly, a previous experience reared its ugly head. Though we knew having children was not going to be of primary importance for our lives together, we decided to try. I was overcome with a joy like no other when, in 2008, Holly presented me with a onesie inscribed with the words "The Clowns Are Going to Get Me" as her way of lightheartedly telling me that we were pregnant. She had such a wonderful smile on her face as I held the onesie up and a tear trickled down from my eye. We were both so happy that we were going to be parents; we just knew it was meant to be.

I was so excited. Over the next few weeks, we were both on cloud nine, collecting books on pregnancy, thinking of names, and deciding how we were going to organize a nursery in our home. I made it a point to let my mother know that we were expecting, and she was genuinely happy that finally I was doing what she had hoped for so long. "It's about time you made me a grandmother!"

With a chuckle, as if this conversation had never happened before, I said, "Well, you're already a grandmother several times over."

In a motherly, matter-of-fact tone, she pointed out, "Well, not from you." I felt warmth that she still pined for me to have children.

Even with the ominous presence from my past that had invaded our home and our lives, we were very happy at having a child. Then, tragedy struck. During what should have been a routine pregnancy checkup, the heartbeat that I recall being so tiny and wondrous was no longer there. We had lost the baby.

I was overtaken with grief. More than being shocked that this was happening once again, I was heartbroken for Holly. I had irrational feelings that there had to be something terribly wrong with me, that I was a complete failure in everything, and now, along with my past failures impacting our lives, Holly was having to suffer this incredible failure I had thrust upon her. I was crushed at how unfair my life was being to her, and I felt helpless to do anything about it. But, with a lot of togetherness, patience, and hope we decided to try again. The result was the same.

I was fearful that the past was definitely going to repeat itself. After two failed pregnancies, I was almost certain that Holly was going to leave me. I was doing my best to avoid these horrible thoughts I had, but one night I couldn't hold my feelings in any longer. The pent-up grief I had tried to hide came rushing out, and I blurted out to her that I knew she was going to leave me because of everything, but now especially because of losing two babies.

With tears in her eyes and an adamant tone, she reminded me, "We told each other early on that we didn't need children to have meaning in our lives. I'm not going anywhere and neither are you." We held each other tighter than we ever had before. I was comforted that neither the past nor anything else was ever going to tear us apart.

Then, in late 2009, life took another difficult turn. That summer, while visiting Miss Helen down in Cape, I'd noticed that she seemed not quite herself. Her speech was somewhat slurred, and she was complaining of weakness in her arms. I urged her to go to the doctor, and she promised me she would—something I knew she would never even have said if she didn't realize that something serious might be wrong.

Over the next few weeks, I stayed in constant contact with my mother about her medical appointments. "I just have arthritis in my throat," was her self-diagnosis, but I wasn't buying it, having spoken with her doctors myself. When the last doctor told her he needed to perform one final test, I arranged for Holly to accompany her, since I had to be in Florida on a business trip.

On the day of the medical appointment, I gave Holly a call to see how it had gone. The slight tremble in Holly's voice told me immediately that the news was bad. "I'm sorry, Jeffrey, but the test indicated that Miss Helen has ALS. Lou Gehrig's disease."

Everything around me just stopped. I knew enough about ALS to know it was fatal and that there was no known cure. "Are you sure? I mean, is the doctor sure?" I desperately needed to hear something else.

"Yes, baby, he was absolutely certain. I'm sorry."

I set about learning as much as I could about ALS—not just to understand it myself but to be able to explain it to Miss Helen. I also made contact with the local office of the ALS Association (ALSA), and I was pleased when they agreed to send two representatives to meet with her.

On the chilly November day when the ALSA staffers arrived, I was there, along with Holly, my brother John, and the usual assortment of local friends who always seemed to be present at my mother's home. The reps brought along packets of information on ALS, documents highlighting the services provided by ALSA, and even a case of Ensure, a dietary supplement that can be helpful for people suffering with ALS.

We sat together in the living room, and the ALSA reps carefully and compassionately explained what we had to look forward to. The sentence that was most important to me was one of the first things they said: "The normal prognosis is about five years after diagnosis." It was painful to think about my mother's death, but I was glad to hear that I could expect at least a number of more years with her.

The reps went on to detail what Miss Helen could expect physically, including the potential need for a feeding tube at some point. As the conversation went on, I could see that Miss Helen wasn't paying very much attention. I sensed that she was putting up with the visitors just to appease me, which distressed me somewhat, but I was comforted by the thought that my brother was there. I hoped that the family would help her get through the hard times ahead with the best possible care. The reps finally departed, with heartfelt thanks from me.

When I ventured into the kitchen, I overheard a comment that disturbed me from one of Miss Helen's oldest friends: "Those white people ain't coming in here telling us nothing. We know how to take care of her."

Trying to remain calm, I entered the kitchen, sat down at the table where my mother's friends were gathered, and asked, "Is there a problem?"

When my question was met with silence, I continued, "Those people were here to help. Do you know anything about the disease she has?" Silence. "Do you?" I repeated. Still no answer.

Now I spoke quietly but firmly. "I know what I'm doing, and I hope no one here is planning to get in the way of what my mother needs."

I left the kitchen and rejoined my mother in the living room, where she was chatting with a couple of other friends. "Mother," I said, "can I speak to you in your bedroom, please?" I think she was moved by the intensity of my gaze. She nodded and followed me.

We sat together on her bed. With as much tenderness as I could muster, I asked, "Mother, do you know what's going on? Do you know how serious this is?"

She looked at me with a smile. "I'll be all right. This will pass. I'll get better."

My eyes began welling with tears. She was reacting with the same kind of denial that Howard had shown when he was told he had pancreatic cancer. "No mother, you're not going to be all right. This is going to kill you. Don't you understand that?" Tears began streaming down my face as I looked to her for a response.

She merely pursed her lips and threw her hands up, as if to say, "So what?"

"How can you be that way?" I cried.

She placed one hand on my shoulder while pointing skyward with the other. "I know I'll be all right because of my belief in Jesus. He will take care of me."

Though I was disheartened at her refusal to accept the assistance I'd offered, I couldn't help being struck by her faith and the strength it gave her. I sensed that, deep inside, she understood what she was facing, and she intended to face it with dignity and courage.

The five years predicted by the ALSA representatives proved to be far too optimistic. Over the next few months, Miss Helen gradually lost the ability to speak, forcing her to communicate using a small dry-erase board provided by ALSA. When we celebrated her birthday on January 24, she was in great spirits, even though she was visibly gaunt and weak. A week later, when she'd gotten to the point where she couldn't even drink the cans of Ensure, she agreed to have a feeding tube put in. Holly and I accompanied her to the hospital, along with other family members. As she waited in her wheelchair for the procedure, she looked up at me with a different type of glint in her eyes—a look of worry that I wasn't accustomed to seeing from her. "It's all right, Mother," I told her. "It's all right." I was scared for her, but also strengthened by her.

The procedure was successful, and she returned home to be lovingly cared for by her granddaughter "Janice." Holly and I would be on call as necessary.

A week later, I received an urgent call from Janice. "Miss Helen isn't doing well," she said. "Should I call an ambulance?"

"Yes!" I replied, and Holly and I immediately jumped into our car for the two-hour drive to Cape.

We arrived at the hospital to find Miss Helen unconscious and having difficulty breathing. The emergency room was filled with family and friends, all looking very concerned. When I pulled the doctor aside, he said that there was not much they could do other than try to stabilize her and keep her comfortable. "She might not make it to morning," he said.

When I took it upon myself to tell everyone else, the news was not taken calmly. My brother John reacted the worst, yelling and pounding his fists on the door until a doctor threatened to have him removed.

I took some comfort when it was decided that she was stable enough to be moved to a private room. I felt proud when one of the doctors commented, "She may not have long to live, but she is hanging on." Miss Helen had always been a fighter, and she was spending her final hours the same way. Holly and I, along with a few other family members, spent a sleepless night in uncomfortable chairs in the waiting room.

The next day finally arrived, and we all made our way to her room, where we were surprised and pleased to see Miss Helen awake and interacting with visitors. I had what would be my last real conversation with her.

"I want to go home," she told me.

"Of course," I said, "as soon as you get better."

Her demeanor completely changed. I couldn't understand what she was saying, but she was pointing a finger sharply at me with a fierce look in her eyes. When I asked, "Are you angry with me?" her gestures became even more intense.

She didn't need to be able to talk. I knew that she was blaming me for the fact that she was in the hospital. It made no sense, but when your mother is dying, logic no longer seems to matter. I burst into tears and fled the room.

When Holly and I returned a little later, my mother looked much worse. The doctor seemed to see the same thing when he came to check on her. "She's suffering from oxygen deprivation," he explained. "She just can't pull in enough, and her systems are shutting down." The oxygen mask they fitted to her face didn't seem to make much difference. Behind her blinking eyes, I got the feeling that she was not really there anymore.

By the time one of the nurses asked to speak with me privately, I was feeling pretty numb.

"Mr. Sterling," she said, "some of the family and friends are complaining that we aren't doing enough for her. A few have been getting a bit belligerent."

I was upset and saddened by what she was telling me, and I wasn't going to let it continue. "If anybody comes to you asking about the care you're providing," I said, "tell them to talk to me." None of

Miss Helen's friends or relatives came to me to complain. I was left to simply wonder which ones were convinced that the hospital was neglecting her.

It was about an hour later that the nurse came to speak with me again, this time with the doctor in tow. "Mr. Sterling," she said, "I'm sorry to say that Miss Helen is getting no benefit from the oxygen machine." I glanced at the doctor, and he nodded in agreement.

I knew what they were saying, even without them having to ask. In a calmer voice than I'd expected, I said, "Please take her off the machine."

"I agree that that is the best thing to do for her now," the doctor said. But as the nurse moved to remove the oxygen mask, my nephew, teary-eyed, cried, "No, don't take it off! Don't do it!" As I glanced around the room, I could see nods and looks of distress on the faces of the others.

Loud enough for everyone to hear, but in a tone that I hoped was steady and calm, I replied, "It's not doing anything for her. There's nothing else that can be done." Distraught, my nephew turned and left the room. I could feel an ice-cold hostility directed toward me from the others. Yet no one said a word.

*They don't understand*, I thought. They didn't understand how tough it was for me when my mother was first diagnosed. They didn't understand why I'd tried to force them to learn about ALS. They didn't understand how painful it is to realize your mother is dying and that almost nothing can be done for her. And they certainly didn't understand how difficult it is to make the right decision when the end has finally come.

At the doctor's suggestion, I agreed to have morphine administered to make Miss Helen as comfortable as possible. Soon thereafter, she died a peaceful death.

A big part of me died with her. But an even bigger part survived.

# CHAPTER SEVENTEEN

# Fate of a Whistleblower

T HE REST OF 2010 PASSED LIKE A BLUR, A THANKFULLY QUIET, even peacefully boring period in my life. It had been four years since the search warrant was executed, and I'd heard absolutely no word from my attorney or the government regarding an indictment or any other legal problems.

The main problem on my mind was my bad knees. I'd been suffering from osteoarthritis for years, and it had now gotten seriously painful. My doctor scheduled my total knee replacement surgery for November—a mild disappointment for me, since it meant I had to resign early as chairman of the employee giving campaign for my region within WellPoint. It was an honor to be selected for the position, and I served to my fullest, even hand-delivering special acknowledgment awards to the top donors, hobbling around on my bad knee. Under the circumstances, it was a relief when I checked into the hospital for the surgery.

Unfortunately, what should have been a routine procedure developed complications, including a blood clot and a problem with the oxygen level in my blood. I ended up spending two weeks in the hospital rather than the normal three days. Afterward, it was good to finally get home, even though I had weeks of painful therapy to endure.

By early January 2011, I was recovering nicely at home, though still experiencing pain and using a cane. On January 6, a Thursday, I received a call from "Dorothy Hogan," now my direct supervisor at WellPoint. She was calling to ask me to attend a meeting with a representative from Express Scripts, the WellPoint pharmacy-benefit management company. Dorothy herself would also attend, flying up from her home office in Georgia. I assumed the meeting related to the work I was doing to combat fraud and abuse in regard to the Medicare Part D drug program.

"Well, sure, I can attend," I replied. "But can it be delayed until Monday? That's when I'm due to return to work."

Dorothy hesitated. "Unfortunately," she finally said, "I have a conflict and can only fly in tomorrow. It's an important meeting, and we really need you there. Are you able to drive?"

"Yeah, I can drive for short spurts. I think I'll be all right driving down."

"That's great. See you tomorrow."

The next morning, I felt pretty good about going to the office. I had been stuck at home for too long; I was eager for a change of scenery and curious to see what kind of work had piled up on my desk. I even enjoyed the commute, though my knee constantly reminded me that I was pushing my recovery schedule a bit.

Walking through the office lobby, I noticed with pride the progress graphic showing how the employee giving campaign for my region had surpassed our goal. I checked in at my office, greeted my fellow investigators, and joined Dorothy in our department's small conference room. I figured that the two of us would soon be departing for the short drive to the offices of Express Scripts. But when I asked Dorothy about it, she responded hesitantly, "Oh, well, we can go up there after lunch."

I returned to my desk and got to work on the pile of correspon-
dence and memos that had accumulated there over the past few weeks.
Just then, my phone rang. It was Dorothy. "Jeffrey, security said there
is an issue with your badge. They need you to come upstairs to the
reception desk."

I was confused. "An issue with my badge? I had no problems coming in today, and they didn't say anything to me then."

"Uh, I don't know. They just said they needed to see you upstairs."

"Well, we'll be leaving for our meeting soon, so I'll just drop by on
our way out." I hung up the phone and continued what I was doing.

After a minute or two, "Peter Fuller," the onetime leader of our
unit, walked up to my cubicle. "Jeffrey, they really want you to come
upstairs."

"All right, all right. What the hell is so urgent? The security office is right there." I pointed to the area where the building's security
staff shared space with us. "Why can't they just pop over here?" Peter
shrugged his shoulders and walked away.

I was feeling exasperated. I had reached my limit for the day walking on my new knee, as the pain was letting me know. But I made my
way up the stairs to the lobby. As I approached the reception desk, the
security officer silently pointed to the visitors' waiting area on the left.

Already approaching me was a group of four people: two uni-
formed St. Louis city police officers, a dark-suited man I didn't recognize, and Ashley K. Hunt, the FBI agent who'd accosted me outside
my home almost five years earlier.

"Jeffrey Sterling," Hunt said, "you are under arrest." The police officers handcuffed me, and Ashley and her fellow agent escorted me to
a black SUV waiting in front of the building. A small handful of news
reporters with notebooks and TV cameras were there too, apparently
having been tipped off in advance by the FBI. I learned afterward that
the reporter for a local news station speculated that my limp might
have been due to a "struggle" with the arresting FBI agents.

My first reaction was total disbelief. It had been so long. So much
time had passed that I'd assumed America was done with me. Now I

realized that I'd been in the crosshairs all these years, and my old feelings of hurt and resentment returned with a horrible rush.

My anger was intensified by the unreasonableness of it all and the sense of betrayal I felt. I hated the fact that WellPoint had participated in this pointless charade, that Dorothy had traveled all the way from Georgia solely to serve me up on a platter to the FBI. There was absolutely no need for such theatrics. Hunt could easily have come to my home and arrested me there, but they had to have their big scene: the public arrest of the traitor Jeffrey Sterling. For Dorothy and WellPoint to have played a part in this circus sickens me to this day.

At FBI headquarters in St. Louis, I was fully processed—fingerprints, pictures, DNA swab, and so on. I remained handcuffed the whole time, sprawled out on a small chair, my leg extended in an effort to get relief from the pain.

"We'll notify your wife," Hunt told me. "Is there anything you want us to tell her?"

I said the only thing that came to mind, "Tell her that I love her."

Next, I was shuffled down to the federal courts building, where I sat and waited for hours. I was so numb, so deeply in shock, that I wished I could cut through my wrists with the grated edge on the handcuffs. It didn't work, of course, but the scratches I gouged lasted for quite a while. I was so distraught that I didn't even realize that Holly was actually in the courtroom during my arraignment.

Later, I was transported to the St. Charles County jail, where I spent additional hours in handcuffs, sitting and waiting. Eventually, I was led to an office to see a doctor—or so they called him—who asked me whether I was suicidal. When I honestly answered "yes," I was placed in one of the special cells set aside for those considered at risk of harming themselves, if not others. My clothes were taken away, and I was given a "turtle suit" to wear—a tear-resistant, one-piece, anti-suicide smock that was apparently intended for a female, because it was several sizes too small. Unable to squeeze into the suit, I had to remain naked, huddling under a blanket on a thin mattress. I was in that cell for over a week.

For the first few days, I refused to eat. The only things that crossed my lips were water and the pills they provided me for pain. I didn't feel I was starving myself; I genuinely had no appetite, and I didn't care about anything other than wanting to be reunited with Holly. But the prison administrators weren't interested in having me die. One of them paid a visit to me and tried to persuade me to eat. "You don't want me to have to tell your wife that you died because you refused to eat, do you?" he asked. I had nothing to say in response.

He also arranged a phone call from Holly, hoping she could convince me. I agreed to speak with her, though I would never have wanted to talk with her under circumstances like this. We exchanged a few words, and the sound of her voice was profoundly comforting, but I continued my refusal to eat, not wanting to provide my jailers with any satisfaction.

When the weekend came, they allowed Holly to pay me a visit. I was thoroughly ashamed at having to wear that tiny turtle suit to see the love of my life. Even the other prisoners expressed embarrassment for me. The glass between us was cloudy and the sound quality of the phone we had to use was terrible. But I could still see how beautiful she was, and the grief in her eyes broke my heart. Holly pledged her love and devotion to me, and I made a solemn promise to her that I would not turn to suicide. It was a promise that would last forever.

After that all-too-brief visit, I told the jailer, "I'll try to eat now if you can bring me something."

A few days later, I was transported to Virginia in handcuffs. A couple of federal marshals escorted me there on a regular commercial flight via American Airlines. The cell conditions in the Alexandria jail were not much better. I was assigned a cell in a high-security block, and my tiny turtle suit was replaced by an oversize green jumpsuit. I found myself thinking that, although I'd ruled out suicide, insanity was beginning to seem like a good alternative.

Now the legal gears of my case began to grind. I was able to visit with my attorney, Ed MacMahon, who informed me that the government was invoking the Espionage Act of 1917 to charge me—a strategy that would enable them to skirt the statute of limitations. In fact, I would eventually become only the fifth person in history to be indicted under the Espionage Act, following in the footsteps of notable figures such as the socialist leader Eugene V. Debs and the anarchist Emma Goldman.

I thought back to something Ed had told me when he'd first agreed to represent me. "I hope you realize that you've pulled on Superman's cape," he said, paraphrasing the lyrics of an old Jim Croce song. I was beginning to understand what happens to people who dare to challenge an entity with superpowers.

Though I had been expecting a sit-down session with prosecutors during these early days of imprisonment, none ever came. The only overture reported to me by Ed was when William Welch, the lead prosecutor, said that they wanted me to "plead to something."

"What the hell does that mean?" I asked.

Ed just shook his head. "I honestly don't know what they're doing," he admitted.

I also had several sessions in front of the judge, Leonie Brinkema. She was a grandmotherly woman with a bun hairdo and a slight stature. I'd spent many years around government types, and she was definitely the type—a bureaucrat dedicated to process and protecting it. At first, she passively accepted every exaggerated and false characterization the prosecutors laid upon me to keep me locked up. According to Welch, I was a threat to society unlike any other. Were I to be released, I might go on a killing rampage directed at the CIA and American citizens in general. Only after two sessions of factual counterarguments by Ed MacMahon did Judge Brinkema seem to grasp that the case against me was more than ten years old and that I had never committed a single act of violence in my life.

Holly was there in Brinkema's courtroom when the motion was made for my release. Accompanying her were our friends, "Andrew and Claire Carter." The moment I'd been transferred to Virginia, they had called Holly and told her that their home was open to her. Holly was staying with them in Reston, Virginia, during my time in the Alexandria jail, and the Carters had generously offered to help us in any way they could. "Is there anyone in this courtroom," Judge Brinkema asked, "who can speak on behalf of the defendant?"

Claire Carter approached the bench. "Judge Brinkema," she said, "Mr. Sterling is very close to me and my family. We can certainly vouch for him."

"Very well," Brinkema declared. "I will release Mr. Sterling into your custody if you agree to provide a ten thousand dollar bond."

Like everyone else in the courtroom, Claire was shocked. She'd been offering her voice in support of having me return home to Holly—not to live in Reston with the Carters. She tried to say so: "I know Jeff would feel terrible about having to stay with us. I know he would much rather—"

Brinkema interrupted with a slight chuckle. "Well, staying with you would be better than staying in the Alexandria jail."

Embarrassed, I looked at Claire with what I hoped was an apologetic expression. But she was already agreeing to meet the judge's demand. As Brinkema rose from her seat and headed toward the exit, I blurted out, "Am I ever going to be allowed to go home?"

Judge Brinkema turned to me with that same smile on her face. "After a while," she remarked, and she disappeared from the courtroom.

# CHAPTER EIGHTEEN

# Show Trial

IT WAS LATE IN THE EVENING WHEN THEY FINALLY RELEASED ME. I ran over to Claire Carter's van, where Holly met me, and I gave her the biggest hug and the warmest kiss ever. I had tears in my eyes all the way to Claire's house, as the emotions I had held in during those weeks of being locked up finally found release.

I had been to the Carters' home many times before, but this time was different. Andrew and Claire had offered to help me and Holly in any way they could, even inviting us both to live with them for an indefinite period of time—a wonderful, generous gift that I will never forget. Holly was able to stay for a few days before having to return to our home and her job, and her comforting presence meant the world to me.

I had to stay in Virginia for more than two months. Judge Brinkema had forbidden me from being home with my wife, near friends and family, despite the fact that no evidence had been presented showing that I was a threat to anyone. She had also required me to get a job while in Virginia, which was basically impossible under the circumstances. I tried to get my old job back at WellPoint, pointing out that my work could be performed from anywhere, and that I still had not been found guilty of any crime. However, it seemed that the adage "innocent until proven guilty" was no longer applicable to me. WellPoint refused to let me come back to work, saying that I'd "quit" by not showing up for work for three consecutive days. It didn't matter that they knew exactly where I was, or that one of their own managers had assisted in my arrest. The blame for my absence had been neatly shifted to my shoulders.

With no hope of getting my job back and the near impossibility of finding a job in Virginia, Holly and I were reduced to living on her salary as a social worker, which was considerably less than what I had been making at WellPoint. I was devastated by not being able to support myself anymore. Our savings were quickly depleted by all the costs of the legal fight, but Holly remained strong and essentially took me on as one of her clients—giving me the emotional, psychological, and spiritual support I needed to survive this latest crisis.

Unable to work, I spent my time in Virginia doing my best to assist my defense lawyers, Ed MacMahon and Barry J. Pollack, who had joined Ed. According to the rules, we could only speak about the case in a sensitive compartmented information facility (SCIF) located in the bowels of the Alexandria courthouse—a small room with barely enough space for a table, set of secure file cabinets, and a computer terminal. It reminded me of the tiny penalty-box office I'd been banished to at the Agency.

As I worked with Ed and Barry, I was shocked by a couple of realities of my case. One was the complexity of the Espionage Act, the 1917 law that the prosecutors had decided to unearth to use against me. Because the law inevitably dealt with classified information, it threw up challenging hurdles in the face of anyone seeking to defend himself against charges under the law. Given that secret information could not be revealed or even discussed in court, my lawyers and I were forced to go into the ring with one arm tied behind our backs.

The other surprise was the paucity of evidence being marshaled against me. There was nothing but conjecture in the form of circumstantial evidence—chiefly phone records that showed I'd participated in calls with James Risen. Risen was the reporter who'd written about my discrimination case for the *New York Times* and the author of the book *State of War*. That book's revelations about Operation Merlin were the basis of the government's case against me. But while I admitted that I'd spoken on the phone with Risen, I denied that those conversations had involved my leaking details about Operation Merlin—and the government had no concrete evidence to show that I'd done so.

"If the jury takes seriously the words 'beyond a reasonable doubt,' then we don't have anything to worry about," Ed told me.

In reviewing the government's case, I also learned that practically every CIA employee I'd ever had contact with had been questioned by FBI agent Ashley K. Hunt. Reading the transcripts of those interviews—in legal jargon, they're known as 302s—I noticed that many of the black employees sounded almost defensive when discussing me. I got the feeling they were disappointed that I was struggling against my treatment by the Agency rather than quietly accepting it, as they had done. They seemed to believe that my troubles were of my own making. They even made a point of volunteering observations as to how and why they found it possible that I was guilty of illegally leaking secret information—never the reverse.

I must point out that a handful of the black employees questioned gave honest, unbiased assessments of me. I'm grateful to those few people, and they have remained my friends.

The FBI interviews of white CIA employees were telling as well. Many expressed their surprise upon meeting me, offering comments like, "I didn't realize he was going to be black," and "You know, there aren't too many black officers involved in these types of operations." It seemed hard for them to get past my color—and the sense that it was difficult for them to trust me came through clearly.

Reading those interviews suggested to me that the trial was going to have only one focus: the battle between a black nonconformist and the American way, as represented by the Agency.

I returned home in April. Holly and I lived through the summer in pained anticipation of the trial, which was scheduled for September 2011. But as the date drew near, there were surprises in store.

One involved James Risen. The government had subpoenaed Risen to answer questions about his sources, but Risen had fought legally against complying with that subpoena. Judge Brinkema had then ruled that the government could not directly ask Risen who his sources were. Now, on a Friday, just three days before the scheduled start of the trial, prosecutor William Welch stated that the government might not be able to try the case without being able to question Risen. He even alluded to the possibility of dropping the case against me.

Another surprise came when Welch revealed at the last moment that the prosecution had learned about government witnesses who could prove beneficial to my defense. This is a violation of the basic principles of jurisprudence. When Ed MacMahon asked Welch to explain the oversight, he replied, "We just got this information from the Agency," as if he was some kind of victim.

Judge Brinkema was unimpressed by this explanation. She ruled that the prosecution could not use the witnesses in question, then ordered that the case be taken off the calendar, effectively ending it.

After adjournment, Holly, Ed, Barry, and I rushed out of the courtroom and made our way to a nearby restaurant to debrief. For the first time in months, I felt hopeful. "Is the case over?" I asked.

Ed shrugged. "It's up to the government. They can appeal, but we'll just have to wait and see."

It would be more than three years before the case was back on the calendar. During that agonizing waiting period, the news media adopted a surprising angle. Although I was the defendant—the person whose freedom was at stake—the press began referring to it as the "Risen case." I became an afterthought, as journalists, TV and radio commentators, and others shifted their attention to the reporter whose sources were still being sought by the government. Many journalists went out of their way to portray Risen as a free-speech martyr being targeted and persecuted by the Obama administration. The news coverage focused on the administration's aggressiveness in going after reporters who used leaked information to expose government malfeasance, especially in regard to intelligence operations. Risen himself traveled the talk show circuit, vowing that he would rather go to jail than reveal his confidential sources. He even received a number of awards for his courage and his principled stand.

All the while, I was feeling practically invisible. I'd lost my job. I'd spent my savings on legal expenses and the cost of travel between my home in Missouri and the courthouse in Virginia, forcing Holly and me to go on food stamps. I was the one paying the price for Risen's supposedly brave stance against tyranny, but the media ignored me. I was alone in challenging the government, while Risen enjoyed the support of his colleagues in the world of journalism. At one time, I'd considered Risen a friend. As time wore on, and I was bearing the brunt of the government's war against us both, it was getting harder and harder for me to think of him that way.

As I'd done during my earlier period of legal limbo, I applied unsuccessfully for a number of jobs. Even the people at the local employment office looked stumped when I walked in and said, "I'll take whatever you have." Finally, Holly came across an ad in the *St. Louis Post-Dispatch* from Serco, a government contractor that had won a bid to run an enrollment center for the new Affordable Care Act, otherwise known as Obamacare. Serco was interested in hiring intake specialists to staff the new center.

When Holly first showed me the ad, I brushed it aside. "No government agency is going to hire me," I said. "I've been accused of espionage. I could never even pass a background check."

"You never know," Holly argued. "Somebody might just look beyond your situation to recognize your abilities and hire you."

I decided I had nothing to lose. Shortly after submitting my online application, I was invited to participate in a group preinterview session. The best candidates would be invited for a second round of interviews. I put my best face forward, and, after a single session, I was surprised to receive a job offer on the spot—contingent on my passing a background check.

Two months passed. I heard nothing from Serco except to be informed that I'd been scheduled to attend a new-employee orientation program. Still wondering what was happening, I showed up on the day when the program was due to start, took part in all the informational sessions, received my employee ID, and signed up for benefits. By the end of the day, my worries had been replaced by welcome relief. Holly and I were both extremely happy that evening.

The next morning, I showed up early for the second day of orientation. I was waiting in the conference room with a cup of coffee when one of the orientation leaders entered with a piece of paper in his hand. "Can I see a Mr. Jeffrey Sterling, please?"

My heart sank. I was taken to the reception area just outside the conference room, where I was met by a Serco manager. "I'm sorry, Mr. Sterling," she said, "but you didn't pass the background check. I'm afraid I'm going to have to pull you out. I think it has something to do with a possible arrest?" She was doing a poor job of feigning ignorance.

"But I haven't been convicted of anything. And that was years ago—"

Before I could say any more, she interrupted me, "I'm sorry. The decision was made at corporate."

The receptionist had already brought my jacket and bag. I left, holding my head high, and went home to Holly.

The next day, while I was cleaning the garage at home, a FedEx truck pulled up and delivered an overnight letter from Serco. It was a form letter with no signature or contact information, letting me know that I had failed the background check. The report was attached. When I glanced at it, I saw that it was dated a month and a half earlier.

Unable to land a job, I toyed around with the idea of going for an advanced degree at Washington University, my former law school.

Maybe this would be a useful way to prepare myself for the eventual end of my legal ordeal. Unwilling to waste time and money on a fruitless application, I visited one of the deans to explain my situation. After hearing about my indictment, the dean remarked, "We'd be hard pressed to turn away a valued alumnus like you," and he promised to discuss my case with his colleagues. I never heard back from him. I guess even law schools don't necessarily lend much credence to innocent until proven guilty.

Eventually the word came down: despite the fact that the government had been unable to force James Risen to give testimony about his sources, the prosecutors were determined to press ahead with their case against me. A new trial date was set, with a preliminary hearing scheduled for January 5, 2015, almost four years to the day after my arrest.

Before the start of the trial, life intervened again. I got a call from my brother John, telling me that our second-oldest brother, Steven, was in the hospital. The news was unclear and confusing, but I gathered that Steve was suffering from liver cancer or liver failure. I was distraught, having always thought of him as the strongest one in the family.

The day before I was scheduled to fly to Virginia, Holly and I drove down to southern Illinois, where Steve was at home receiving hospice care. I was taken aback by his gaunt look and swollen legs. I held my anguish in, trying to offer him as much comfort and support as I could.

Just before I left, Steve surprised me by asking about my situation—a topic my brothers had usually ignored or avoided. I explained that I was heading off to the trial.

"You don't give up, you hear me," he said. "You stay in there and fight." It was Steve talking, but I also heard Miss Helen's voice in those words. I left with a new sense of resolve.

As before, I was required by Judge Brinkema to reside with the Carter family when I was in Virginia, and, as always, they welcomed me into their home. Holly was scheduled to join me in a few days.

On Monday, January 5, 2015, James Risen was called to the stand. The goal was to allow Judge Brinkema to preview what Risen was going to say if prosecutors ordered him to testify about the sources of his reporting. Risen's replies were consistent: "I am not going to provide the government with information that they seem to want to use to create a mosaic to prove or disprove certain facts," he said.

As for the prosecutors, they didn't press Risen to reveal his sources. Instead, they asked him merely to confirm some basic facts that he'd already revealed—for example, that his book relied on unnamed confidential sources, and that he'd interviewed me for the 2002 article about my discrimination case.

It was an odd charade. My legal team ended the day confused as to what the government was going to do next. The prosecutors had said at one point that they had no case without being able to question Risen about his sources. So now, with their star witness making it clear that he would refuse to testify, and the government itself refusing to press him on the issue, was there going to be a trial or not?

That evening, I was at home with the Carters, updating them on the day's craziness, when Holly called. Claire answered the phone, and her face quickly turned somber. When I spoke to Holly, I understood why.

"I'm sorry, Jeffrey," she said, her voice full of emotion. "Steve died today."

The day had started off as a circus and ended in tragedy. I suddenly felt more exhausted than I had in a very long time.

Judge Brinkema delayed the trial by one day so I could attend Steve's funeral.

When the trial began, I really had no idea what to expect. I took what solace I could from steadfast Holly, who sat behind me every day. The look of the jury was not very comforting. There was not a single black person among them, and the middle-aged women who filled the front row of the jury box looked harsh and unsympathetic—like the white people I'd met from time to time who made no bones about declaring they were "tired of black people playing the race card."

The trial seemed to me to be a kind of CIA showcase. One by one, my former colleagues, managers, and coworkers were paraded in front of the jury members, who were visibly impressed by the fact that they were seeing and hearing actual covert CIA officers talk about their work defending America. The Agency employees testified to the fact that they had had access to me and to information about Operation Merlin, which they considered the most important CIA operation of the past generation. Most described me as a good officer. However, Jerry, the former head of the New York office, repeatedly characterized me as a "deficient" case officer, though he was at a loss to explain why a deficient officer was involved in such a significant operation. The complexities and virtues of Operation Merlin were front and center; details regarding officers, tradecraft, sources, and methods were served up willingly by the government in its case against me—despite the fact that my own discrimination case against the Agency had been stymied by the supposed national security threat posed by the unavoidable discussion of CIA operations the trial would have entailed.

My discrimination case, in fact, played an odd role in the espionage trial. One of the strongest objections entered by the prosecution came when Ed and Barry tried to point out that, at the time the leak happened, my discrimination case was still ongoing. This puzzled me at first. Then I realized the reason the precise timing was important to the prosecution: they wanted the jury to believe that I'd leaked the information because of my bitterness over losing the discrimination case. Judge Brinkema upheld the objection.

As the days went by, it was impossible not to notice the racial subtext of the trial. Every officer called to testify against me was white, while I was the lone black officer involved with Operation Merlin. Perhaps it was to counterbalance this one-sided impression that the government decided it was important to display a different sort of black face. They called to the stand former national security advisor and secretary of state Condoleezza Rice. She did a fine job in her star turn, proclaiming how vital Operation Merlin had been and how well it had been managed. The members of the jury were clearly smitten that such a famous person was there to testify against me. Rice's testimony capped the argument being constructed against me by the Agency: Operation Merlin was a successful project that might have been very effective in blocking Iranian efforts to build a nuclear weapon, had it not been for the disgruntled officer who'd wantonly destroyed the operation through his malicious and illegal leaks.

During the second week, the two Senate staffers to whom I'd conveyed my concerns about Operation Merlin were called. One was Donald Stone, who'd led the interview with me, then failed to write a report about our meeting until several weeks later, after the FBI had started its investigation. The other was Vicki Divoll, who'd also been present during the meeting. She'd left her job at the Senate in 2000 under somewhat mysterious circumstances, and stories had been circulating that she'd been fired as punishment for having leaked classified information to James Risen herself. (She denied these stories when they were raised by my lawyers in a filing related to my case.) Divoll seemed nervous on the stand, constantly blinking her eyes and stuttering.

As the trial continued, I gradually came to the realization that when I'd made complaints to the two congressional committees, I'd been speaking with people connected to the CIA rather than disinterested third parties. No wonder my complaints had gone nowhere—except to be used, now, in the legal case against me. The feeling grew in me that, from the moment I'd first complained about being subject to racial discrimination, a machine had begun to be assembled with the singular purpose of destroying me. It seemed I had to be punished for my attempts to make inroads into a world where I did not belong. Every day during the trial felt like a reenactment of my recurring nightmare. The forces arrayed against me were so big, while I was a tiny wanderer, struggling to make my way against a vast, opposing sea.

Of course, that's how it appeared from my personal, very subjective perspective. To an outside observer, the picture appeared quite different. Near the end of the trial, Ed MacMahon told me, "They haven't laid a glove on you." Maybe he was simply trying to bolster my morale.

If so, it didn't work. Regardless of the facts presented in the court-room, I was still a black man sitting in the defendant's chair. Under the circumstances, it was impossible for me to feel optimistic.

The prosecution rested its case, such as it was. Feeling that I didn't even know what I was supposed to be defending myself against, I didn't take the stand myself. Instead, we called only one witness: Benjamin Lewis, the father of Cindy Carlson, whose baby I'd watched as the nanny. While living with the family, I'd used a PC that Benjamin had given them. Part of the government's evidence had been a blank file on that computer titled "merlin." The prosecution assumed that the empty file must have been where I stored secret information about Operation Merlin. However, they never bothered to check that as-sumption. In court, Benjamin testified that he'd previously used the computer for his business, and that the "merlin" file had held a pro-ductivity program sold by a company called Merlin Business Software. There was no connection to the CIA at all. It was just another example of the absurdity of the prosecution's case.

With that, the defense rested. I waited for a decision—and, I hoped, an end to the nightmare.

# Epilogue
## After the Verdict

T HE SENTENCE HANDED DOWN BY JUDGE BRINKEMA CALLED for me to serve forty-two months in prison. It was a longer sentence than the one imposed in other similar cases, such as that of John Kiriakou, who in 2012 had become the first former CIA officer convicted of giving classified information to a reporter. Perhaps even more egregious, just a month before my sentencing, General David Petraeus, a former CIA director who'd confessed to giving classified documents to his biographer, Paula Broadwell (who was also his long-time mistress), had been permitted to enter a plea bargain with federal prosecutors that would require not a single day in prison.

Brinkema justified my harsher treatment by saying that I'd failed to "own up to what I did." Her statement made it clear that she'd never seriously considered the possibility that I might be innocent. As far as she was concerned, the trial was just a set piece that had to be tolerated in order to uphold the image of equal justice.

Two months later, on June 16, 2015, I self-surrendered to the federal prison known as FCI Englewood in Littleton, Colorado. The plane trip and subsequent car ride to the facility with Holly somehow seemed both excruciatingly long and painfully short. By the time Holly had to leave me there, she had tears in her eyes, while I felt all teared-out. I'd developed a feeling of acceptance for the inescapable ordeal I now faced.

Prison was exactly what I expected it to be, closely resembling the facilities I'd been incarcerated in for shorter periods along the way. There were strict racial dividing lines everywhere, from the television rooms to the cafeteria tables, enforced subtly by the prison officials and more blatantly by the inmates themselves. FCI Englewood was a low-security facility, which primarily meant that most of the doors and windows had no bars. Guards and prisoners alike considered Englewood "easy time"—just "some time away from your family," as one inmate described it to me. I took no solace in that. It was still prison—a symbol of banishment and removal from the country I loved and had tried to serve, a reminder that there was no place in either white America or black America where I was welcome and wanted.

I was also struggling with the label that had been pinned on me in the news media: whistleblower. It was a better label than criminal or traitor, but I wasn't sure it applied to me. Based on high-profile cases like those of Edward Snowden and Chelsea Manning, most people had the impression that whistleblowers are those who illegally leak secret information to the press in an effort to expose governmental wrongdoing. That was more or less how I was characterized in my trial, yet it wasn't the truth about me. I'd tried to draw attention to CIA malfeasance using the methods prescribed by law: I'd sued the Agency for racial discrimination, brought my complaints about the same discrimination to the House Intelligence Committee, and tried to warn policymakers about the dangerously flawed Operation Merlin by going to the Senate Intelligence Committee. Unlike Snowden or Manning, I hadn't taken the law into my own hands. I'd followed the rules, only to end up being punished for it. I believed, and still believe, that the distinction is an important one.

But, in the end, I came to embrace the label of whistleblower. My methods were not the same as those of other whistleblowers, but my goal was parallel to theirs: to right a wrong and stand up for the principles of justice and integrity that are supposed to define America. I was a whistleblower for my country. And I am proud of that.

It seems especially ironic that I was prosecuted for being a whistleblower—and a rule-obeying one, at that—by an administration many people considered progressive and strong on human rights. Barack Obama is widely regarded as a world hero, and as our first black president one might assume he would be sensitive to the realities of racial discrimination. Yet those realities seemed to have had no impact on his treatment of me, or on the policy decisions made by his attorney general, Eric Holder—another black man. Before leaving office, Obama would see fit to pardon James E. Cartwright, a former Marine Corps general who'd been convicted of lying to the FBI about his discussions with reporters regarding Iran's nuclear program. Obama also commuted the sentence of Chelsea Manning. No such act of mercy would ever be offered to me.

Like it or not, this was the reality I had to deal with. I settled into prison, feeling as dejected and miserable as I'd ever felt in my life. If not for my promises to Holly, I'm sure the temptation of suicide would have loomed large in my consciousness.

Then, in the midst of the worst depression I had ever experienced, something wonderful happened. The letters started coming—messages of support and solidarity from people I'd never met from all over the world.

Actually, such messages had begun to trickle in even before my sentencing. In the days after my conviction, I'd heard from friends I had lost contact with over the years, as well as family members who I'd thought were unable to understand and accept me. Many of them lined up to write letters to Judge Brinkema on my behalf. I was absolutely floored when I learned that Archbishop Desmond Tutu, a legendary leader of the South African movement against apartheid, had also written a letter about me to Judge Brinkema (see below). Although Tutu's appeal for a fair sentence for me had failed, this gesture by a champion of civil rights from another country helped make up for my disappointment over being disregarded by civil rights leaders from my own land.

Dear Judge Brinkema

The ideals that we share for the rule of law and equal justice are often confronted by the cynicism that says such virtues are not to be fulfilled in the real world. So we are challenged to prove such cynicism wrong. It is in that context that I am respectfully writing to Your Honor about the sentencing of Jeffrey Alexander Sterling.

Equality under the law, as a cornerstone of justice, is significantly at stake in the sentencing of Mr. Sterling. While I realize that no two cases are identical, the fact remains that charges akin to those for which Mr. Sterling was convicted have in recent years resulted in extremely disparate penalties. An editorial by the *Los Angeles Times*, dated March 5, 2015 and titled "A Double Standard on Government Secrets for David Petraeus," summed up an assessment made not only by that newspaper's editorial board but also by a wide range of well-informed observers in many walks of life. The editorial concluded that vastly harsher punishments for those who have divulged classified information while lacking the high rank and power of former CIA Director Petraeus "may be the way of the world, but it's not justice."

Your Honor, I appeal to you to provide the sentencing of Mr. Sterling with a sense of equity that can help to move the way of the world closer to real justice, nurturing belief in the law as a guardian of justice and not a violator of it. I hope that you will pronounce a sentence for Mr. Sterling that is consistent with our aspirations for equal justice under the law.

*God bless you*
*Archbishop Emeritus Desmond Tutu*

Now, during my months in prison, other letters of support addressed to me began to arrive—first in a trickle, then in a near flood.
They were the result of Holly's tireless efforts to call attention to my
plight. She'd given interviews, made speeches, and even led a march
to the White House to deliver a petition containing thousands of sig-
natures asking for my release. People around the country, moved by
her appeals, took it upon themselves to reach out to me. I felt a tinge
of embarrassment during prison mail call as my name was called for
letter after letter, provoking understandable envy from my fellow inmates. Many of my well-wishers wrote letters designed to remind me
about the things I had to look forward to after prison—gardening,
travel, home-cooked meals, and other simple pleasures of freedom.
Some sent me books on anything and everything you can imagine; I
learned more about topics like haiku and chickens than I would have
ever thought.

Having interesting things to read is a critical respite from prison
life. But for me, those letters and books were much more than just
an escape. They represented the kind of hope I'd given up on. The
America of acceptance that I had fought to discover my entire life was
reaching out to me at the time when I needed it most.

>‹‹

AFTER TWO AND a half years, on January 16, 2018, I walked out of
prison and into Holly's warm embrace. As she drove me to the airport
for our flight home, Holly—doing her best to fight back her tears—
asked me, "What would you like to eat?"

I'd been dreaming for a long time about the first fabulous meal
I would enjoy once the prison gates were behind me. But when the
moment came, I could only think of one thing. "Orange juice. I would
really like a glass of orange juice."

Holly was as surprised as I was, but such is the shock of freedom.

On the quiet two-hour flight home, the emotion of the day took
its toll on Holly. She drifted off to sleep clutching my hand as if she
would never let go again. As for me, I felt a sense of release like never

before, mingled with a quiet satisfaction that I'd survived the horrendous journey I'd so frequently dreamed about. There was no dark, shapeless room of despair to fear any longer. I'd survived black and white America, and persecution as a whistleblower, without sacrificing my belief in myself. I reflected on the many times when I could have simply given in, surrendered, or accepted the limiting expectations of others. But I'd resisted those temptations, and I'd survived.

Flying high above the country that I'd always longed to be a part of, I thought of a letter written by James Baldwin, one of the authors whose writings I was happily reintroduced to in prison. "A journey," Baldwin wrote, "is called that because you cannot know what you will discover on the journey, what you will do with what you find, or what you find will do to you."

I've been on a hell of a journey, and it's not over yet.

# Acknowledgments

FIRST AND FOREMOST, I WANT TO EXPRESS MY SINCEREST thanks to my wonderful wife, Holly. She has been my biggest fan and staunchest supporter through both good and bad times. She inspired me to revisit and finish this book.

Writing this book has been a dream come true, and I am eternally grateful to my agent, Laura Gross, for believing in me and my story and helping this book become a reality. I have learned what a daunting task it is to write a book, especially a memoir, and I am indebted to editor Karl Weber for keeping my story focused and adding clarity to my writing, and to Katy O'Donnell and Bold Type for remaining patient with my unique writing circumstance.

To those who fought at my side, including but not limited to my legal dream team of Edward MacMahon Jr. and Barry Pollack. To the countless supporters who helped me survive prison: your sentiments and support opened my eyes to the America I never knew but always believed existed. Special thanks to Norman Solomon and Archbishop Desmond Tutu for the incredible benevolence shown to me.

I also thank family and friends who have all been part of my journey. Having you in my life has made me a better man, and I hope I have been a comparable and worthy brother, relation, and friend. My story would not have been possible without you.

Last but not least, I want to thank Miss Helen, my dear mother. I am saddened that she is not here to read this story, because she started it all for me. She inspired me to make the journey that is life on my terms. I love and miss her.

# Index

**JEFFREY STERLING** is a former CIA case officer who was at the Agency, including on the Iran task force, for nearly a decade. He studied political science at Millikin University and holds a law degree from the Washington University School of Law in St. Louis. He currently resides with his wife, Holly, and their two precocious kitties in Missouri.